The Reminiscences of

Rear Admiral Thomas J. Hamilton

U. S. Navy (Retired)

U. S. Naval Institute
Annapolis, Maryland
1983

Preface

In the realm of college football, Rear Admiral Tom Hamilton's name is a well-known one. He played for Navy's 1926 national championship team, coached the Midshipmen in the mid-1930s and mid-1940s, served as athletic director for the Naval Academy and later the University of Pittsburgh, and was commissioner of the Pacific Eight Conference. He has been elected to the National Football Hall of Fame and holds a number of other honors attesting to his success in sports--as player, coach, and administrator.

He had another successful career as well, as a naval aviator. In the years before World War II, he flew several different types of aircraft: torpedo, scout, patrol, and transport. During the war he served as air officer, executive officer, and temporary commanding officer of the famous USS Enterprise, one of the top aircraft carriers of the war. He also commanded the escort carrier Savo Island briefly at the war's end. In the period at the beginning of the war, Hamilton combined his two principal interests while heading the Navy's pre-flight training program. Recognizing the value of competitive sports in preparing men to be naval aviators, he worked with Captain Arthur Radford to establish a rigorous sports program which paid dividends once the men received their training and reported to the fleet.

REAR ADMIRAL THOMAS JAMES HAMILTON
UNITED STATES NAVY (RETIRED)

Thomas James Hamilton was born in Hoopeston, Illinois, on 26 December 1905, the son of John L. and Mary Hall Hamilton. He attended Indianola School, Columbus, Ohio, and Doane Academy, Granville, Ohio, before his appointment to the U. S. Naval Academy in 1923. While a midshipman, he won letters in football, baseball, and basketball, was president of his class, and as a first classman had his name engraved on the Thompson Trophy Cup as the midshipman who had done most during the preceding year to promote athletics at the Academy. He was also awarded the Navy Athletic Association Sword for general athletic ability and leadership. Graduated and commissioned ensign in June 1927, he progressed in rank attaining that of captain on 20 March 1945. He retired from the Navy on 1 February 1949, when he was advanced to the rank of rear admiral on the basis of combat citations.

After graduation in 1927, he remained at the Naval Academy for Aviation instruction, and the following December joined the USS Maryla He served in that battleship for two years with the exception of the football seasons of 1927 and 1928, when he had temporary duty as assistant coach at the Naval Academy. Ordered to the Naval Air Statio Pensacola, Florida, for flight training, he was designated Naval Aviator on 28 July 1930, then again served as assistant football coach at the Naval Academy until the following December.

In January 1931 he joined Torpedo Squadron One, based on the aircraft carrier Lexington, and in June 1932 was transferred to Scouting Squadron Six, aviation unit of the cruiser Milwaukee. While so assigned he was head football coach of the U. S. Fleet Team on the Pacific Coast during the seasons 1931, 1932, and 1933. From 1934 unti 1937, he had duty in the Department of Physical Training, Naval Academ with additional duty in 1936 as Instructor in Aviation for Midshipmen From March 1937 to early 1940, he served in squadrons of Patrol Wing One as gunnery officer, and made flights from the mainland to Hawaii, Alaska, and the Caribbean. For two consecutive years his squadron received awards for highest standing gunnery competition.

In June 1940, he reported as Assistant Operations Officer at the Naval Air Station, Anacostia, D. C., and from July until December 1941 was Operations Officer of that station. He next served as Officer in Charge of Preflight and Physical Training Section, Aviation Training Division, Bureau of Aeronautics, Navy Department, Washington, D. C., where he was in charge of organizing and developing physical training programs for Naval Aviation cadets entering the service for the first time. He was awarded a Legion of Merit with the following citation:

"For exceptionally meritorious conduct in the performance of outstanding services to the Government of the United States as Officer-in-Charge, Physical Training Section, Naval Air Training Division, Bureau of Aeronautics, December 1941 to June 1943. Charged with the difficult task of preparing a thorough physical and indoctrination program for air cadets, Captain (then Lieutenant Commander) Hamilton formulated effective plans and was responsible for the selection and establishment of the first four as well as other Pre-Flight Schools at which approximately 250,000 cadets received ground training and the physical conditioning essential for combat. He selected and indoctrinated approximately 2,100 officers for teaching in the schools and other aviation units of the Navy. In addition, he was instrumental in establishing the Naval Recognition School at Ohio State University. His untiring efforts in training skilled airmen, his administrative ability and unwavering devotion to duty reflect the highest credit upon Captain Hamilton and the United States Naval Service."

When detached, in June 1943, he reported for duty as Air Officer on board the aircraft carrier *Enterprise*, and from June to December 1944, as her Executive Officer, he participated in the invasions of the Gilbert and Marshall islands, and all engagements in the Battle of Leyte Gulf. For his services during this period he was awarded the Bronze Star Medal, with Combat "V," and the following citation:

"For meritorious service as Executive Officer of the USS *Enterprise*, during operations against enemy Japanese forces in the Philippine Islands Area and the Battle for Leyte Gulf from August 30, 1944, to October 25, 1944. Displaying sound judgment and professional skill, Captain (then Commander) Hamilton rendered invaluable assistance to his commanding officer throughout the hazardous missions of the *Enterprise* and materially aided his ship and air group in successfully repelling numerous hostile air attacks and inflicting great damage on enemy ships, aircraft and shore installations. . ."

Detached from the *Enterprise* in December 1944, he joined the staff of Commander Air Force, Pacific Fleet, in January 1945. For his services as Air Force Training Officer, he was awarded a Gold Star in lieu of a second Legion of Merit, with the following citation:

"For exceptionally meritorious conduct in the performance of outstanding services to the Government of the United States as Force Training Officer on the Staff of Commander Air Force, Pacific Fleet, during operations against enemy Japanese forces in the Pacific War Area from January 20 to October 1, 1945. Demonstrating outstanding ability, Captain Hamilton established facilities to provide each man in every branch of the Fleet's aviation organization with a thorough knowledge of modern war equipment. In addition, he supervised the development of new techniques of solving the maniford problems incident to a constantly expanding aviation organization and aided in the integration of a complete training program for pilots, aircrewmen and all other aviation specialists, thereby contributing materially to the superior record of the Air Force, Pacific Fleet. . ."

In October 1943, he returned to the United States and reported to Commander Training Command, Pacific Fleet, as a prospective commander

R. Adm. Thomas J. Hamilton, USN (Ret.)

of an aircraft carrier escort. He assumed command of the USS Savo Island on December 1945. On February 5, 1946, he was again ordered to the Naval Academy for duty this time as Director of Athletics and Head of the Department of Physical Training, a post he held until his retirement on December 31, 1948. Soon thereafter he accepted a similar position at the University of Pittsburgh, in accordance with his desire "to devote all his time to the development of youth."

In addition to the Legion of Merit with Gold Star in lieu of the second Legion of Merit and the Bronze Star Medal, with Combat "V," Rear Admiral Hamilton has the American Defense Service Medal, Fleet Clasp; the American Area Campaign Medal; the Asiatic-Pacific Area Campaign Medal, with engagement stars; and the World War II Victory Medal.

His official residence is 224 15th Avenue, Columbus, Ohio. He is married to the former Miss Emmie S. Spalding of Coronado, California. Their two sons are Thomas James Hamilton, Jr., and William Howard Hamilton.

Navy Office of Information
Internal Relations Division (OI-430
9 March 1964

DECLARATION OF TRUST

The undersigned does hereby appoint and designate as his (her) Trustee herein, the Secretary-Treasurer and Publisher of the United States Naval Institute to perform and discharge the following duties, powers, and privileges in connection with the possession and use of a certain taped interview between the undersigned and the Oral History Department of the United States Naval Institute.

1. Classification of Transcript.

(X)a. If classified OPEN, the transcript(s) may be read or the recording(s) audited by the qualified personnel upon presentation of proper credentials, as determined by the Secretary-Treasurer of the U.S. Naval Institute.

( )b. If classified PERMISSION REQUIRED TO CITE OR QUOTE, the user will be required to obtain permission in writing from the interviewee prior to quoting or citing from either the transcript(s) or the recording(s).

( )c. If classified PERMISSION REQUIRED, permission must be obtained in writing from the interviewee before the transcribed interview(s) can be examined or the tape recording(s) audited.

( )d. If classified CLOSED, the transcribed interview(s) and the tape recording(s) will be sealed until a time specified by the interviewee. This may be until the death of the interviewee or for any specified number of years.

2. It is expressly understood that in giving this authorization, I am in no way precluded from placing such restrictions as I may desire upon use of the interview at any time during my lifetime, nor does this authorization in any way affect my rights to the copyright of my literary expressions that may be contained in the interview.

Witness my hand and seal this 4th day of December 1978

Thomas J. Hamilton

I hereby accept and consent to the foregoing Declaration of Trust and the powers therein conferred upon me as Trustee:

B T E Bowen Jr

Hamilton #1 - 1

Interview with Rear Admiral Thomas James Hamilton, USN
(Retired)

Place: 7580 Caminito, La Jolla, California

Date: April 21, 1978

Subject: Biography

By: E. B. Kitchen, CDR., USN (Retired)

Q: I wanted to put on the tape that you have a beautiful home and that your lovely wife is here and that the Institute, I know, is very pleased to have you take the time to do this recording for us.

Adm. H.: Thank you. It's a pleasure to have you here and to try to conform to this interview. I'm flattered by being asked.

Q: I think we might as well just start at the beginning. Tell me something about your early days, perhaps the influences in your life which led you to take the course which you have.

Adm. H.: I grew up in a large family, born in Illinois in a little town called Hoopeston and we moved to Columbus, Ohio when I was about seven. I had a wonderful dad and mother. My dad was a prominent banker. He was at one time president of the American Banker's Association in 1905. I was the youngest of five sons and we had a very happy childhood. With five boys in the family it was pretty active and I grew with a great interest in sport around our activities right in the household, and being closely associated with Ohio State University where all my brothers went. They were active in sports so I had that normal interest.

One day when I came home for a weekend from Doane Academy which was a prep school in Granville, Ohio, my brother John who'd been in World War I in field artillery, a captain, asked me if I would like to go to the Naval Academy. I said, "Well, I don't know." He said, "You look into it because I think I can get you an appointment if you want to go." So, I went across the street to a Mrs. Hudson, whose son had just graduated from the Naval Academy, and borrowed a Lucky Bag for the class of 1922. I saw in that Lucky Bag all the wonderful sports programs at the Naval Academy, so I told my brother, "Yes, that's where I'd like to go."

So, I can't boast of a long term ambition to be a naval officer when my interest first was aroused by sports. Of course, I loved the Naval Academy and the Navy so you don't have to know exactly that you want to be a naval officer. Sometimes you'd come in for other reasons and find

Hamilton #1 - 3

out that you like it.

Q: Isn't it somewhat of a cliche that the best naval officers come from the mid-west, where they didn't see the water before?

Adm. H.: That's been said - I don't know whether that's true, but they get a large proportion of the midshipmen from the mid-west, so some of the best at least would come from there.

Q: I think we ought to put on the tape just for record purposes the date of your birth.

Adm. H.: December 26, 1905 which I've been told is probably the worst birthday of the year -

Q: The day after Christmas, of course.

Adm. H.: I've always had a very good time about it.

Q: Maybe this resulted in a double celebration.

Adm. H.: I realized when my brothers had birthdays, I wondered where mine went. It was all involved in Christmas.

Hamilton #1 - 4

Q: I know you had an extremely active part in athletics at the Academy and it would be very interesting to have you describe your participation in sports while you were there.

Adm. H.: I enjoyed the whole four years at the Naval Academy. I think plebe summer is a very important time for midshipmen. You get acquainted with your classmates and we had about a thousand who entered and we had 574 who graduated which shows you the attrition that took place in those days. Actually I enjoyed plebe year. It's supposed to be difficult but having been raised in a kind of competitive family, I found plebe year a continuation of so-called kidding and joshing and educational things, which I'd gotten from my older brothers and I found it was a very enjoyable year, as were the others.

During all four years I was interested in sports and played on the football, basketball and baseball squads. I made nine varsity letters and enjoyed my experience very much. We were fortunate in having a very successful year, my first class year, due I think to the input of leadership that came with Admiral Jonas Ingram who was a captain at that time, and Director of Athletics, and his brother, Bill Ingram, who came in as football coach and who has been one of my idols ever since. He was a great man and a great football coach. That season brought us the national championship, at least in the eyes of most of the people in the United States, though I have found that on the West Coast sometimes Stanford debates the title. But it was a great year and we revenged a bad licking that we had taken from Michigan the year before. They were the champions in the Big Ten that year and we also beat Purdue which was second in the Big Ten. We had good victories over Princeton, Colgate, Georgetown and other teams, so that we ended up for the Army game undefeated, and this game was played in Chicago to dedicate the new Soldier's Field which had been built out there. This is the only time that the Army/Navy game has been played away from the East Coast. It drew the largest crowd that had ever seen a football game - 110,000.

Q: Even including today?

Adm. H.: That's right. It was quite a classic game ending 21 to 21. Army had lost only one game to Notre Dame, 7 to 0, so the game was billed as the championship deciding game. They had Harry Wilson and Kris Cagle and Hewitt and Chic Harding and an end named Gar Davidson whom I later had many dealings with. The game ended in a tie, 21 to 21, and we had of course one of the greatest all-Americans, Frank Wickharst, our captain at one tackle and Tom Eddy at the other tackle.

Hamilton #1 - 6

Q: What position did you play?

Adm. H.: I was a halfback that year and then we had Ben Born and Johnny Cross, guards, and Whitey Lloyd and Hank Hardwick at the end. Jack Hoerner and Wendell Osborne at center and we had Howard Caldwell, Jimmy Schuber, Ned Hannagan, Mo Goudge, in the backfield. We enjoyed playing together. They've all been great friends of mine through my life.

Q: You had some awards during the time that you were at the Academy. Would you care to mention those and tell me why you were so great and got them?

Adm. H.: I was selected to some of the all-American teams that year, and Frank Wickharst was consensus all-American. Tom Eddy also received selections. My last year I was captain of the basketball team and played under Johnny Wilson, who was a wonderful coach. We won 15 and lost two games that year, so that was a very successful season and in baseball I was catcher and we had a good season that year.

At the end of the year the Thompson Cup, which is awarded to the midshipman who supposedly has done the most for athletics at the Academy during that year, was given to me and I also got a special sword for achievement

Hamilton #1 - 7

in athletics which I very much appreciated.

Q: Did you hold any class offices?

Adm. H.: Yes, I was class president from the time they first elected one in youngster year, and our class was very lazy, because they failed to elect anybody else, so I've held it for 54 years.

Q: That's a wonderful story. What was the size of your class upon graduation?

Adm. H.: Five-hundred, seventy-four.

Q: You had said it started at a thousand some and then that was the attrition. Almost half of them fell by the wayside.

Adm. H.: Yes, I think it was typical in those years. Maybe the Navy thought our class a little out of balance - our class was so much larger than previous classes. They turned back quite a few of our class into '28. We had a very good relationship with '28 with quite a few who were just put back a year.

Q: And you then became an ensign and -

Hamilton #1 - 8

Adm. H.: Became an ensign in 1927 and then following indoctrination summer at the Naval Academy in aviation, six of us were kept on as assistant coaches in football.

Q: What was the aviation instruction like in those days?

Adm. H.: They had patrol planes and –

Q: This is at the Academy?

Adm. H.: At the Academy, operating out of Severn River and Chesapeake Bay and they would take four or five of us in each one of the patrol planes and give us the rudiments of how they flew the plane. We fired the machine guns and did some navigation and just got our feet wet a little bit trying to find out what it was all about. It interested many of us, who elected to become Naval aviators.

Q: Who did the piloting of the planes?

Adm. H.: They had regular Navy officer pilots who were in the squadron.

Q: I see.

Adm. H.: Later on when I went back to coach in '34, I was

Hamilton #1 - 9

an instructor in aviation.

Q: I see, I see.

Adm. H.: And gave the same kind of training to the midshipmen.

Q: But it was just barely getting your feet wet, because that ended in December, I think.

Adm. H.: Well, it ended actually in the summer - it was only about a six week course. I then was an assistant coach to Bill Ingram in football that fall. I enjoyed another season there and had the good opportunity to work with Joe Clifton, who was sort of my protegé as he followed me as line backer. I became very close to Joe Clifton.

Q: What was his nickname?

Adm. H.: Jumping Joe.

Q: Very colorful man.

Adm. H.: Yes, he was, and he turned out to be a very colorful admiral in the Navy.

Q: Did you do as many ensigns did and get married the day after you graduated?

Adm. H.: No, I did not. I didn't get married for five years. I left the Academy and reported aboard the USS Maryland at the Bremerton Navy Yard just before Christmas in '27. I enjoyed my duty aboard there as a junior officer, served as a junior officer on the broadside battery, and then as a spotter and then as an assistant turret officer. Then I went back to the Naval Academy the following fall again as football coach. Ben Born and I coached the plebe team that year. We formed very close associations with the Class of 1932 which included Magruder Tuttle, Lou Bryan, Lou Kirn, Joe Tschirgi, and other great young men who were in that class. We have enjoyed their friendship ever since.

Q: What was the luck you had with your teams while you were an assistant coach? Were they as fortunate as you had been?

Adm. H.: That plebe team won all its games except one - Kiski School beat us 7 to 6.

Then I went back to the Maryland and after a time I got a turret, number four turret, on the ship. Commander Oscar Badger was the first gunnery officer and athletic officer, and I coached the basketball and baseball teams there. Then Commander Harry Hill relieved him and Jerauld Wright was also on board. Each later were famous admirals. I was lucky to be under them, so I enjoyed my stay on the Maryland.

In October of '29 I had orders to Pensacola and went there for flight training.

Q: Did you apply for that? Did you want to go there?

Adm. H.: Oh, yes, I was very anxious to be a flier. I applied and in due time got orders.

Q: The exposure right after you graduated caused you to continue with your aviation duties, I presume.

Adm. H.: I think that helped a great deal, yes. The training at Pensacola was a very thorough and enjoyable time. In the following fall, 1930, I was ordered back to the Naval Academy again as assistant coach -

Q: Had you finished your aviation training by then?

Adm. H.: I had my wings and I think my number as an aviator was 3,042 to complete the course, the number in naval aviation. I was assistant to Bill Ingram again

Hamilton #1 - 12

that fall of '30 and then following that reported to Torpedo Squadron 1 at North Island.

Q: That was in January of '31, I think?

Adm. H.: January of '31 and we prepared to go aboard the Lexington for fleet exercises which took place that winter.

Q: I wanted to ask, on the Maryland you said you joined her in Bremerton. Were your duties mostly on the West Coast and what were your duties, I should say - I mean what was the Maryland doing at that time.

Adm. H.: Well, she was in the battle force, one of the latest battleships that we had and we were involved in all the maneuvers and battle practices that were carried on at that time. The fleet was very competitive, in peacetime. The fleet was competitive in gunnery, engineering, communications and also in athletics which I'd like to bring up later. The ships were involved in very busy schedules competing with one another, which is excellent training. Then we had various cruises to Hawaii and other places, but all on the West Coast.

Q: So then when you came back to the fleet again you were still on the West Coast aboard the Lexington in

Torpedo Squadron 1, is that right?

Adm. H.: That's right.

Q: Tell me about that.

Adm. H.: We were involved in carrier operations. To me, they were fascinating. There were all sorts of carrier landing drills and qualifications that had to be carried out before the fleet cruise, a rugged training schedule which I enjoyed. The cruise that year was to Panama. In one of the Fleet exercises they pitted the Lexington against the Saratoga and Langley, which were the opposing carriers. Captain King was skipper of the Lexington and a brilliant man.

Q: The captain later to be the Admiral King?

Adm. H.: Yes, Ernest King. One afternoon he launched his whole air group against the opposing force about three or four in the afternoon and we caught the other task group by surprise. They didn't expect us late in the afternoon and supposedly it was a very successful attack. We reformed and headed back for the Lex but unfortunately when we got to the spot where we thought the Lex was, we didn't see it. We were looking for the ship and we re-checked our navigation. We knew where we were but we missed her. None of the air group had qualified at night landings aboard ship. We'd had night bounce drill on the field. The situation was quite grim. We circled and the Group Commander, after we'd been lost for a period of time, formed a scouting line west and just as darkness came we saw a searchlight beam. It was the _Lex_ and it certainly looked good. The whole air group raced for the carrier. Some of the fighters had only a quart or a gallon of gas in them; they were very close to running out of fuel but everybody got aboard without a single accident. That was the first night landings any of us had had aboard a carrier.

Q: Incredible, isn't it?

Adm. H.: Yes.

Q: How many were in total, do you recall? How many were there of you?

Adm. H.: I think there were 72 planes in the group.

Q: Goodness, so it was dark by the time all of them got aboard.

Hamilton #1 - 15

Adm. H.: Many of the people of that flight remembered it very well.

Q: I should think.

Adm. H.: Cliff Cooper was one whom I see occasionally.

Q: That was certainly learning the hard way, wasn't it?

Adm. H.: That's right but I think it illustrates the ingenuity and initiative and the aggressive frame of mind of Admiral King. Really, I think we were fortunate to have a man of his stature in the position he held during World War II.

Q: But you spoke of going to Panama, did you come close to the Canal at all?

Adm. H.: Oh, after that exercise we went through the Canal, and we operated in the Caribbean and we had exercises all during the winter. We flew over to Managua carrying supplies when they had the earthquake over there. It was a very interesting cruise.

Q: Well, there was no trouble on size at that time of the carriers getting through the locks and through the Canal.

Adm. H.: There was just a foot clearance on both sides for the Lexington and Saratoga.

Q: Is that right.

Adm. H.: It was a very tight squeeze but they made it. Incidentally I guess coming two days after the Senate vote, I might be allowed to say that I regret very much to see the United States pass over the control of this vital waterway to Panama. I feel that we should have had a better negotiation and treaty, which would possibly make us partners with Panama, but not for a giveaway such as we've done.

Q: There are a great many people in the United States who would agree with you on that opinion.

Adm. H.: I find that there are a great many, mostly Navy people that I've talked to feel that way.

Q: And that's a good picture of your operations while you were on the Lexington. Was Admiral King in charge all the time you were aboard?

Adm. H.: Yes, he was.

Hamilton #1 - 17

Q: You weren't there very long, were you? Well, let's see what, a year and a half you were on -

Adm. H.: I was there a year and a half. Then in those days they used to transfer you to different types of aviation duties to give you experience, and I was transferred to a scouting squadron aboard the Milwaukee which was a light cruiser and that was a good experience also.

Q: I forgot to ask you what kind of planes were you flying off the Lexington?

Adm. H.: We first flew TMs which were the old Martin torpedo plane and then we went back and picked up TGs which were the Great Lakes torpedo plane built in Cleveland, Ohio. They were lumbering old planes which everybody would probably laugh at today, but they carried a torpedo or bombs and we got a lot of good experience flying them.

Q: And you were the aviator on that? You were the number one aviator on the plane?

Adm. H.: Yes, that's true. There was a crew of two pilots and a gunner and a radioman, so there were four in the plane.

Hamilton #1 - 18

Q: What did the G stand for?

Adm. H.: Great Lakes.

Q: Oh, Great Lakes, I was thinking Grumman.

Adm. H.: Well, in those days - I don't think the corporation lasted but -

Q: There was a corporation called the Great Lakes?

Adm. H.: Great Lakes Aircraft Corporation and it was probably absorbed by one of the other companies.

Q: I see. Then what on earth did airplanes do on a cruiser?

Adm. H.: They were used for scouting and for observation. First we had O2U3s which were a Vought plane which could operate either on wheels or you could put a float on it and operate at sea. Later we got OJ planes, the J being for Berliner-Joyce Corporation. Again, a light two-seated observation plane and we were catapulted with a powder catapult from the cruiser. It seemed they always fired you on the down roll but we always got a good push to get launched. When you came in to land, the ship would make a slick by turning rapidly and you'd come down and land in that slick while it lasted and then be hoisted aboard by a crane.

Q: You say you were hoisted aboard by a crane?

Adm. H.: Yes, we'd taxi alongside the ship and the crane would train out and you'd hook on and be hoisted aboard.

Q: How many planes were on the Milwaukee?

Adm. H.: Two planes. They were used to spot gunfire and also for searches and for observation.

Q: That was a different kind of experience, wasn't it?

Adm. H.: Oh, yes.

Q: I wouldn't like that hoisting aboard a bit!

Adm. H.: Well, it wasn't bad.

Q: It wasn't.

Adm. H.: Sometimes if it were a little rough, you had to be very careful as you taxiied alongside and also after you got hooked on, you had to be steadied by hand lines.

Q: I would think there would be a danger of crashing into the side of the ship.

Adm. H.: They used a kind of long pole suspended from the ship and then we had these lines to both wing tips for steadying after you were hooked on.

Q: Well, you had some other interesting experiences. I don't want to interfere with having you tell me of other experiences while you were an aviator on the Milwaukee, but I wanted also to talk about your coaching in those days.

Adm. H.: During that time I had temporary duty in the fall from the Lexington and from the Milwaukee to coach the U.S. Fleet team which was formed under Commander Oliver (Scrappy) Kessing who had been graduate manager at the Naval Academy and who organized this Fleet team. The Army, the West Coast Army, had won the series for six years playing the championship battleship team and the Navy was tired of losing and so they put together a fleet team by taking the best players from all the ships teams. We had a marvelous squad. The West Coast Marines also played and we had a good competition for the President's Cup.

Q: United States president?

Adm. H.: The United States president had a cup for the service championship of enlisted teams. I had played in one of those in 1928, for the Newport training station team after completing coaching the Plebe team there at the Naval Academy. Ben Born and I were sent up to Newport and we played the Quantico Marines and we won the President's Cup that year. These three years out here were a valuable experience to me as a coach. We had a marvelous squad of football players to work with and we had very successful seasons. We beat the Marines three times, beat the Army twice. The Army quit the last year and wouldn't play, but we did win from the Marines those three years and we also played a very representative schedule. One of the few games we lost to the University of California at Berkeley with Bill Ingram coaching there, 12 to 7 in 1932.

Q: He was coaching at Berkeley?

Adm. H.: Yes, and so that was -

Q: How come? Had he gotten out of the Navy and -

Adm. H.: He was a civilian coach at the Naval Academy. He had resigned after he graduated the Class of 1920, but he left the Naval Academy as coach in 1930 and came to California and coached there.

Q: I see.

Adm. H.: So this renewed the friendship when I competed against him.

Q: And rivalry as well.

Adm. H.: He was very nice to us; he allowed us to practice on the field with the University of California and I felt badly that they beat us that day because I thought in our practices we were better than they were. We played the Olympic Club, Loyola University, University of San Francisco. Then we played collections of all-stars from USC with some of their famous players and we won those, so it was a successful venture and I'm so proud of all those enlisted men. Only one of them did not receive a commission during World War II and all of them had distinguished careers as officers in World War II.

Q: That's very noteworthy, isn't it?

Adm. H.: Yes, it is.

Hamilton #1 - 23

Q: How many would there have been in the group?

Adm. H.: We had a squad of 55 and much as I loved the Naval Academy teams, I never had a squad at the Naval Academy which matched in manpower for brute strength and size with the fleet team. We had some big horses and they could run.

Q: Did any of them enlist because of their athletic prowess? Or would you know?

Adm. H.: I think so. The Navy used to have a very outstanding athletic program, and I might as well make the point right here. I put it down as a recommendation later on. I believe now that the Navy is in a peacetime era, they should come back and build an attractive athletic program and competition in their service units. The Navy athletic program has really deteriorated a great deal. They seem to think they are upholding morale in the Navy by getting them out to the beer parlors and the massage parlors as fast as they go on liberty. I think they should have some activities which are normal to young men of their age in the schools, high schools, and colleges, of the country where they have representative teams with a chance to develop their skills, they have pride in their teams. In the old days the Ironman competition for overall athletic competition was very bitterly fought out amongst the ships of the Pacific Fleet.

You'd see a ship's personnel betting a whole month's pay on a baseball game. Maybe that wasn't a good feature, but it showed the intensity with which the men felt in those teams. It also gave a verve to life in the Navy that I think is needed. I think it should be well considered to reinstall a more attractive and fulsome program than they have now.

I notice the Navy had a seminar recently on the habitability aboard ship and about nutrition and food servings for men aboard ship, which is very good, to increase the living satisfaction. But why not a competitive sports program which gives incentive and satisfaction -

Q: Certainly builds morale.

Adm. H.: That's right.

Q: Is the Navy program now pretty much defunct or -

Adm. H.: Well, it's largely intramural and almost within small areas. They have a few competitions, but it's my impression that it's inadequate.

Q: But it gave you the opportunity also to deal with the

civilian side of athletics on the West Coast and you took your teams in to the places, the locations of the schools and played on their fields. Is that right?

Adm. H.: That's right. We played the colleges and people knew about us. We were on the sports page, which talked about Navy programs and I think it interested young men to join the Navy, because they would have opportunities to play sports.

Q: Seems to me it's an obvious PR ploy anyway.

Adm. H.: I think it is. Maybe it's one of those things, where the old days are better than now, but I really think it should be considered and I have a book here, put out by Commander Andy McFall, who was fleet athletic officer I think in '32. It shows the number of teams that each of the ships supported and what great interest they generated - rowing races with whale boats and cutters. They had all sorts of competition.

Q: Well, that's very interesting.

Adm. H.: That was the point I was going to bring up later.

Q: Well, do make it and I think we want to go into it

even more so when we're talking about the training which you participated in BuAer in early '41. I want to have you expand on it if you will, please.

Adm. H.: Fine.

Q: But you were on the <u>Milwaukee</u> for three years, is that right?

Adm. H.: No, let's see, it was two years. In the spring of '34 I was ordered back to the Naval Academy as head football coach. The experience that I picked up out here was very valuable to me, and perhaps was not without notice. The Navy made me head football coach at the Naval Academy and I had the opportunity to go there.

Q: Before we go on with that did you - was the coaching for the Pacific team a full time job?

Adm. H.: No, it was part time. During the fall months I would not operate with the squadron.

Q: I see.

Adm. H.: It would be about three months that I missed in the squadron, but I flew some, during that time.

Q: I see because the Milwaukee - on the Milwaukee it was - you were part of a cruiser scouting squadron 6, I believe.

Adm. H.: That's right and we had two other aviators, Andy Jackson and Joe Young. I missed out about three months of it.

Q: I see so it was football season that you were absent.

Adm. H.: That's correct.

Q: Well, obviously it did stand you in good stead since they wanted you to come back to the academy.

Adm. H.: It was - I've had these mutual interests of flying and coaching all along, so to go back there is a great honor. We had a fine season in '34, with a very alert and intelligent group. The players were small but spirited and we had a couple of good advantages. Buzz Borries, the halfback was probably the greatest back that I've ever seen. He had the ability to change pace and speed in running with the ball, he could pass, he could kick and he was almost the whole pass defense in himself, the safety man. We had a superb punter in Bill Clark and then we had a great tackle in Slade Cutter and some very alert, sharp young people like Dusty Dornin and Dick

Burns and Zabriski and Lambert and Tommy King and Dick Pratt.

At any rate, we had a good season. Up to the next to last game we were undefeated and then we played Pittsburgh for the championship of the east and Pitt had a powerhouse, one of the best teams I've ever seen and they beat us 31 to 7. I think we'd have done better if we had gotten the ball, but we couldn't take the ball away from Pittsburgh.

Q: It would have helped, wouldn't it?

Adm. H.: Yes, so then we ended up the season with the Army/Navy game as always, and we won it 3 to 0 on Slade Cutter's place kick, in the mud. That was very noteworthy because it was the first time Navy had defeated Army in thirteen years. So we enjoyed that very much.

Q: Was that your last year there as coach?

Adm. H.: No, that was my first year.

Q: Well, that was quite an accomplishment, wasn't it?

Adm. H.: It was a good year and we were ranked number 3 in the country as a team, in national rankings. We graduated quite a few after the first year. The next year we played more people because they were about even in ability. We had a good team. I think we won five and lost four, but we lost to Army. That was bad news. Gar Davidson, who I mentioned before and who I played against in 1926, was the coach at West Point as he was in '34.

Q: I see.

Adm. H.: Then in '36 we beat them again and we had a 6-3 season. We won from Notre Dame two out of three years. The football squads were a great bunch of football players and midshipmen who became and have been great Naval officers and Marine officers during later years. It was a fine experience for me.

I also served as an instructor in the patrol squadron and Naval Academy instruction in aviation during those years -

Q: Would you be the coach during the football season and then do aviation instructor duties for the rest of the year?

Adm. H.: Coaching duties took up most of the year. In the summertime I would fly the midshipmen. They had a midshipman indoctrination course.

Q: Like you had taken when you were -

Adm. H.: That's right.

Q: You were now teaching what you had taken before?

Adm. H.: Yes, that's right. They had other planes at the Academy for flying but the instructional work was mostly in patrol planes. So I was able to keep my hand in flying during that time.

Q: Were there other athletics than the football? Would you participate in coaching them?

Adm. H.: No, football held my entire time outside, of a little bit of aviation. We were starting a recruiting program, which you have to do in football in collegiate ranks. We helped to organize new chapters of the alumni association so we would get more contacts in various parts of the country. We were trying to get athletes interested in coming to the Academy. I can always recall one athlete who we thought might win an Army/Navy game by just his ability alone. He had about a 3.6 average in his academics and he was about 210 pounds, 6' 3" and a wonderful quarterback, but he was color blind. They would not approve him physically for failing a color blind test. Bill Nicholson was this young man's name. He went on to play center field for the Chicago Cubs. Had a red baseball been thrown at him, he would not have seen it. A white one he used to knock out of the park.

Q: Isn't that interesting?

Adm. H.: A great young man who wanted to be a Naval officer, too.

Q: Sometimes one wonders about the restrictions as applies to entry qualifications, if they are completely logical.

Adm. H.: Well, it's important to recognize a red and green light.

Q: That's true when you're driving a car that's for sure.

Adm. H.: But I think there are branches of the Navy such as Supply Corps or Engineering Duty Only and a lot of other specialties where that requirement is not necessary. Also, if a person is color blind, he can always have somebody beside him who can see the lights.

Q: I think that has been modified to some extent.

Adm. H.: I think it has too.

Hamilton #1 - 32

Q: Do you like to teach?

Adm. H.: Oh, yes, I like to teach and I think coaching is teaching.

Q: That's what I meant actually.

Adm. H.: But take a normal officer's duty aboard a ship or a squadron, he is teaching all the time. He has to keep abreast of the developments and explain what the equipment will do and how to use it. This is going on all the time. I think a large part of the duties of a Naval officer is that of a teacher.

Q: Learning yourself and teaching others.

Adm. H.: Yes.

Q: What did you do - how did you approach the problem of morale? I'm sure that was a big factor in your winning teams?

Adm. H.: Every coach has a different method but I think you have to be yourself. I think some of the Notre Dame people who followed Rockne all tried to copy him and some of them couldn't do it. They weren't themselves. Each coach has to be natural and find his own way of dealing with people. Sometimes he has to be tough; sometimes he has to be easy, but he must apply it individually. I think Bill Ingram was a great model for me. He was a marvelous coach. He was tough but he was gaining your trust and building your incentive. My theme song was "Confidence." I don't think you can do anything unless you believe you can do it. I stressed that point.

Q: Who were some of the great coaches? This probably is extraneous but I'm interested in the athletic aspect of your career, the great coaches in civilian life in those days. Was Vince Lombardi then - ?

Adm. H.: Oh, no, he came on later. He was an assistant at West Point to Red Blaik when I coached at the Academy in '46 and '47.

Q: I see. You can see what I know about coaching, sorry about that.

Adm. H.: I knew Vince. He was a good coach, a good line coach. Red Blaik, of course, was a top man, excellent, and he had Vince as one of his assistants. Vince learned a lot from Red Blaik. Each had his method. Lombardi was a very rugged individual and called a spade a spade.

Hamilton #1 - 34

Q: I think what you make the point is remarkable that everyone does his own thing. If you try to copy someone else, you're pretty much lost because you have to do it your own way and as far as confidence in individuals -

Adm. H.: You learn from others but you've got to do it naturally.

Q: I guess that applies to everything, doesn't it?

Adm. H.: I guess it would, yes.

Q: Well, let's see now. Will it be interesting to talk about your - the next three years then. You had the patrol wing one of a gunnery officer, right?

Adm. H.: Yes, I left the Naval Academy in January 1937 and I came to San Diego in VP9 squadron. We had PMs which were the old Martin patrol planes at that time, prior to taking delivery on a brand new patrol plane then, the PBY which were built right across the bay here in San Diego by Consolidated Aircraft Corporation. This was a marvelous plane to us. We had a hot plate; we could cook food. The flying boat had good range and was a comfortable plane to fly. Those were interesting years because we did a lot of exploratory work in the patrol field.

Our squadron took part in the first mass squadron flight from San Diego to Pearl Harbor which took us twenty-two hours. We delivered those planes there. Later we had another flight out to deliver more planes and it was a twenty hour flight. During fleet maneuvers we had a flight from San Diego to Panama which lasted twenty-five hours. That was a good long stretch, especially when we had bad weather along the way. During that fleet exercise we operated out of Panama and San Juan, Puerto Rico and then proceeded up to Norfolk. It was a good cruise that year.

Also, during the summers of '37 and '38 our wing was embarked in survey duty in Alaska and the Aleutians trying to pick out possible bases for our Navy. A war with Japan.

Q: They had none up to that point?

Adm. H.: The Navy had a partial base at Sitka. We flew to Kodiak, where a fine site was evident at Womens Bay. Adak and Dutch Harbor were already picked out but we did survey work connected with them.

Q: What was the name of the Bay?

Adm. H.: Womens Bay.

Q: Women?

Adm. H.: There is a famous river that empties into the Bay. It's called the Buskin River which was one of the famous fishing streams in the world at that time. I think it still is.

That was interesting duty. During that time, Admiral Ernest King, was our fleet airwing commander. He was a very aggressive, stern boss, but I think good for us. To illustrate the point, I recall we were in Sitka with two squadrons - two squadrons were in Kodiak. All four squadrons were to fly the next day to Seattle. The two squadron commanders in Sitka went to Admiral King and said, "The weather's going to be bad tomorrow, let's go today. We can get in some night flying and it could be a good exercise and we'll avoid the bad weather." Admiral King said, "No, we're scheduled to go tomorrow, we go tomorrow."

Q: Was he then a commander?

Adm. H.: No, he was an admiral.

Q: He was an admiral then?

Adm. H.: Yes, a rear admiral and he had command of the four squadrons in the fleet airwing. So, the next day there was a pea soup fog right on the water. We had a foul weather doctrine of take offs every two minutes on a certain course, at a certain rate of climb, at a certain air speed and were directed to join up on top. Well, Admiral King elected to go in my plane and so I lost the assistance of my second pilot. He was Sandy Heyward who later became Chief of Bureau of Personnel. We took off under that doctrine and on the climb up our plane hit a slip stream which was kind of scary to me. I eased off a little bit in course and rate of climb and took what I thought was a safe path to get out of any slip stream and hold relative position. About 13,000 feet we picked up a load of clear ice. Now there are three types of ice. Clear ice is the worst and most dangerous. We had no deicing equipment aboard the PBY1. The propellers threw ice and broke the navigational compartment windows and took away our radio antenna.

Admiral King pointed that the air speed meter was going down, and I pointed to him that there was a big glob of ice on the pitot tube which controlled it. Promptly, I nosed the plane down and found a slice of air between cloud strata at about 5,500 feet where the ice melted. We continued on the course on which all planes were going to join up on the way to Seattle.

Q: Had you lost contact with all the other planes?

Adm. H.: Yes. We didn't see anybody. After a while there was a little dim disk of a sun in the overcast overhead, and I asked Sandy if he would take an octant sight of the sun and get us a line of position. He did and he handed a note with the position forward. It showed us between Queen Charlotte Island on one side and the mainland of Canada on the other. I gave it to Admiral King. He said, "It can't be, I gave orders we're going down seaward of Queen Charlotte Island."

Well, about a half hour later we came out of the clouds, Queen Charlotte Island on one side and the mainland of Canada on the other, so Sandy Hayward's line of position was correct. It was a scary flight and when we all landed, there was a feeling of relief evident when we had cocktails together at Sand Point air station.

Q: Everyone made it?

Adm. H.: Yes, everyone made it. Gus Kaspararek had a forced landing but he got rid of his ice on the water and took off again.

Q: Oh, he did - he landed and then took off?

Adm. H.: Yes, he landed in the open sea into the prevailing wind and got away with it. At the party Admiral King was talking to a bunch of us and he turned to our squadron commander, Red Tomlinson, and said, "Well, Tomlinson, what were you thinking about up there in that weather?" Red said, "Do you really want to know, Admiral?" The admiral said, "Yes." Red said, "Well, admiral, I just wondered if you knew enough to be scared!"

Q: What was his reply, do you remember?

Adm. H.: I don't remember that. Admiral King was trying to improve the standard of performance in instrument flying under all weather conditions. In some of the exercises right off San Diego in poor weather, we had a couple of bad crashes. Red Hutchinson and Elmer Cooper were lost with their plane crews when two planes collided. Some pilots gave up their wings after that.

Q: That was during this tour of duty?

Adm. H.: Admiral King insisted we fly under any conditions, which brought up the standard of flying performance a great deal. It was needed.

Q: To his credit, he didn't send someone that he didn't go on himself.

Adm. H.: That's right. Admiral King then showed the same qualities which he displayed during World War II.

I understand that it was at Admiral King's insistence that the U.S. fought wars in the Pacific while engaged in all the fighting in Europe. Had he not insisted that the United States go into Guadalcanal and try to hold back the Japs, we would have not had a foothold and Australia would have been lost during World War II.

Q: I think history proves that to be the case.

Adm. H.: I think this had been documented, so I'm an admirer of Admiral King. I think he was a hard taskmaster but a great leader.

Q: You flew to Hawaii on two occasions. Wasn't that fairly soon after the first Pan Am flight had made it to Hawaii?

Adm. H.: They were the early days of the trans-Pacific crossings, I think Pan Am was flying the clippers about two years before those flights. These were exercises by the Navy, the first patrol squadrons who flew over.

Q: That would have been within a period of three years before -

Adm. H.: 1937 along in there.

Q: I believe the Pan Am first flight was '34, wasn't it?

Adm. H.: I don't know exactly but I think that's approximate.

Q: So you came very early in the long distance flying game.

Adm. H.: These were the first mass flights for the Navy in the patrol planes. Admiral Rodgers, of course, tried many years before with one patrol plane. He had a forced landing and was lost for two or three days before discovered. I've forgotten what year that was, but I would think it was about '31 or '32.

Q: I see. You were a gunnery officer, were you not, in patrol wing?

Adm. H.: Yes. That was my department job there, working people out in the Norden bomb sight. We also held gunnery school and were influential, I think, in getting the side gun blisters put on the PBYs. The patrol planes were largely indefensible, but at least the blister improved the defense over the previous machine gun installations that we had.

Hamilton #1 - 42

Q: Explain that, will you?

Adm. H.: In the waist gun hatches, any time anybody would try to train around a fifty caliber machine gun, he would hit the back of his head and shoulders against the turtle-back of the plane, so he couldn't really fire effectively. So, in cooperation with Consolidated we designed a blister which extended the fifty caliber gun out farther, and gave the gunner room to rotate behind the gun over a large arc. This improved his aiming ability.

Q: So you were actually three years in the patrol squadron and you did the long distance flying and you had the gunnery school, also?

Adm. H.: In the fourth year I was transferred to Captain Mason's staff of PatWing 1 and I was gunnery and operations officer for the wing.

Q: I have information that you were - your squadron received awards for the highest standards in the gunnery competition for two consecutive years.

Adm. H.: We did in bombing and machine gun practices that we had. That's part of that fleet competition I was talking about. One squadron competed against the other under gunnery rules. The rules gave a bonus for those squadrons in high altitude bombing for altitude. The higher you bombed, it gave a multiplying factor to your scoring. There were two theories. The planes had no oxygen equipment, but we trained for about a month in our squadron at 17,000 feet which is the maximum altitude of the plane. Our squadron people were nuttier than fruitcakes from flying every day and bombing at that altitude without oxygen. The other squadrons trained at 10-12,000 feet, and then the final day we would go up for the top altitude. I think our getting used to being at that altitude, without oxygen, helped us. Our squadron did win the bombing competition that year.

Of course, now they have oxygen so it is not relevant now. But those kinds of things - one squadron would pit their theories against another on how to do things, to win the competition.

Q: Was that off the coast here?

Adm. H.: We bombed at San Clemente island which is 90 miles from North Island where we were based.

Q: How many of you were involved?

Adm. H.: We had an eighteen plane squadron, and had

probably 180 men in the squadron I would say.

Q: And did you tell me who was the commanding officer at that time?

Adm. H.: Our first skipper was Commander Tomlinson.

Q: Oh, he was the same one -

Adm. H.: Yes, Commander William Gosnell Tomlinson and he was succeeded by Commander Buddy Braun who was a great ordnance expert. Then Al Olney relieved him.

Q: While you were gunnery officer.

Adm. H.: Yes, that's right.

Q: But aviator as well, no?

Adm. H.: Yes, I was a pilot of one of the planes. The pilots in the squadrons have collateral duties in charge of one department or another.

Q: And your gunnery school was ashore over at Terminal Island.

Hamilton #1 - 45

Adm. H.: At North Island.

Q: North Island. Well, you found that interesting duty, though.

Adm. H.: I enjoyed that. I think naval aviation is probably the most desirable thing you can do and the greatest job in aviation is to be skipper of a carrier. A carrier requires the greatest teamwork of any organization I know of.

Q: We want to talk about that a little later, expand on it. I hope you will. And so from there what happened?

Adm. H.: In 1940 I was ordered back to the naval air station Anacostia in Washington, D. C. with Red Tomlinson, my ex-skipper. I was assigned to the Operations Department. Our duty was to have planes ready for the aviators located around Washington to fly. Also we flew a lot of transport planes where we took VIPs, Mock-up boards, various admirals, congressmen, on official trips around the country. It was excellent experience in airline flying. We also took delivery on new aircraft that were manufactured on the East Coast. That was interesting. We would fly to say, Bethpage, pick up Grumman planes, or Buffalo, to pick up the Curtiss dive-bombers, or Newark for Brewster fighters.

We'd fly them back to Anacostia, outfit them with radio, and prepare them for ferry flights to the squadrons on the East or West Coast, wherever they were to be assigned.

It gave one an opportunity to fly almost everything the Navy had. The test section of the Navy was at Anacostia in those days so we saw all the experimental planes that came in there and sometimes were able to fly them. We met a lot of interesting people. I used to fly Secretary Forrestal quite a bit and Secretary Knox, Admiral Stark and many congressmen. Here is an interesting story about Lieutenant Commander Buck James of the Class of '32 who came in from the fleet and reported in as one of our transport pilots.

I had to check him out in a Lockheed Lodestar plane. You had to check each pilot out.

Q: You didn't do it yourself, did you?

Adm. H.: Oh, sure.

Q: You did it personally.

Adm. H.: I was operations officer. Part of that job was to check the new pilots out in our planes and I was involved in the transport flights also. I saw right away that Buck could fly the Lodestar beautifully and needed very little familiarization work. So he did some landings and take-offs. The next step in training was to take a short trip. So, when the next day we got a request from Norfolk, "Please send transport plane to pick up VIPs," it was a perfect training flight for Buck James. He went to Norfolk, and time went on with no report of his departure. Well, about two in the afternoon word came that our air station was closed. Nobody could come aboard or leave.

Q: Which air station, Norfolk or Anacostia?

Adm. H.: Naval air station Anacostia, our own, and we tried to figure out what that was about. No report on Buck. Later we found out that President Roosevelt was coming over to meet this plane. I started to worry a little bit because time was going on and Buck had had no night landings in the Lodestar. After dark we got the departure report, Lieutenant Commander James, Norfolk to Anacostia and we notified the White House. Soon President Roosevelt's car drove up to the operations line and we met him. Fairly soon we lighted up the field and in the meantime I wasn't telling anybody about Buck!

Q: I wouldn't have.

Adm. H.: So we lighted the field and in comes Buck. He

puts the plane down in, just a perfect landing, and taxies up to the operation line. Who should step out but Winston Churchill!

Q: How had Winston Churchill gotten to Norfolk?

Adm. H.: I don't know, but he probably came by ship.

Q: I presume then that the cover had lifted somewhat where earlier in the day when it had said no take-offs or landings at all.

Adm. H.: Well, this was just security for President Roosevelt.

Q: Oh, I see, I see. I thought it was the weather but it was because of security.

Adm. H.: This was a sideline on this type of duty. At least we saw and met Mr. Churchill and saw him meet the president.

Q: Of course, Lieutenant Commander James knew who he had on board. It must have given him some concern to realize who he was carrying and had never made a night landing.

Hamilton #1 - 49

Adm. H.: Buck was a very confident pilot and officer and I don't think it really bothered him at all.

Q: He'd been taught to believe in himself, obviously. Well, that's a wonderful story.

Adm. H.: Well, those were very interesting times.

Q: Was President Roosevelt able to get out of the car and meet him, do you remember?

Adm. H.: No, he stayed in the car and Mr. Churchill got in the car with him.

Q: Let's see, that would have been in the early 1940s, wouldn't it?

Adm. H.: That would have been in '41, because when Pearl Harbor hit we were involved immediately in flying fuses in our transport planes to the West Coast. Apparently there was a shortage of fuses so -

Q: Wasn't that dangerous?

Adm. H.: I guess they might have gone off it you'd had an accident with them. I came back from a flight and had notice to report to Captain Radford. I'll call him admiral because later he became one of the great ones, but he was a captain at that time. He was Director of Naval Aviation Training. He explained to me his idea that he wanted to use competitive athletics and training in athletic skills to increase the abilities of combat pilots for the Navy. He felt that the use of various sports could quicken the eye, improve the judgment, the reaction time, get better mobility and precision and also teach necessary skills like swimming to our pilots, because these pilots would have to fly most of the time over water.

I told him that I concurred completely and thought these methods would be a valuable addition to the present training.

Q: What was his job at the time he asked you about this?

Adm. H.: He was Director of Aviation Training in the Bureau of Aeronautics under Admiral Towers.

Q: I see, and had war started by that time? Had Pearl Harbor –

Adm. H.: Yes. Pearl Harbor had happened when that conversation took place.

Hamilton #1 - 51

Q: I wanted to pinpoint it.

Adm. H.: He had been thinking about it I guess. He asked if I thought we could get good coaches to come into the Navy to teach this sort of thing. I said, yes. I suggested he send someone to the joint meeting of the NCAA and the American Football Coaches Association to tell them the idea and find out who would want to serve.

Q: Excuse me now, had you been detached as operations officer and sent over to do anything else, or were you still operations officer?

Adm. H.: I was still operations officer. After that conversation, I made another trip and came back. There was another note to report to Admiral Radford. He said, "I'm ordering you to go out and make this presentation to the coaches and NCAA." As a coach, I had some previous knowledge of the people and had a lot of acquaintances there. So, I did make the trip to Detroit and made the presentation to the assembled group. The reaction was very good and many spoke right away that they'd like to serve. I told them to get their applications in to the Bureau of Aeronautics.

I took the train back to Washington and went to work the next day at Anacostia. Who should be there, but Bear

Bryant. He was then the assistant coach at Vanderbilt University but now, of course, is one of the foremost coaches now located at the University of Alabama. He said, "I heard your talk, and I'm ready to go to war." I said, "I will see that your name will be one of the first to be considered, but I have nothing to do with it except to make the presentation. You go back to Nashville and I'll make sure you're called among the first selected. Within the next week I received orders to come over to Admiral Radford's staff and was put in charge of the Pre-flight Schools and the Physical Training section. I'd been in this job less than a week when who should show up again but Bear Bryant. He said, "I haven't heard from you! I have left home; I'm not going back. I can't go back now; I've told all my friends that I've gone off to war." So he lived in our home for about three weeks and we put him to work answering the phone and working as a civilian until we could finally process him and get him in the Navy.

Incidentally, we were very careful about selection. We selected about 2,500 officers out of 25,000 applicants and this process got the top coaches and physical education professors in the whole nation. They came in the Navy and wrote up the syllabus of our physical training. They designed it around what the aviator does, and how sports could improve those skills. For instance, gymnastics and tumbling were one of the sports. This was to get the candidate or cadet used to being in all kinds of attitudes, upside down, tumbling for acrobatics and so forth. Soccer was quite an important one, not only for conditioning and competitiveness, but for use of both feet which an aviator uses on the rudder bar. We had wrestling, hand to hand combat. Probably the most important sport we taught was swimming, where the flyer was going to need good ability. In the final check-out tests, the pilots had to swim a mile. Often times they were taken out to sea a mile and dumped overboard and swam ashore.

The pilots and air crews took long hours of the swimming training plus a lot of other activities such as survival. We commissioned twin brothers, the Craigheads, who were survival experts for the National Geographic Magazine. They wrote the book for the Navy on survival and survival training. This was part of the required course. Later on the Craigheads, both lieutenants, went out to an uninhabited island in the South Pacific and lived for a month without taking any food. They lived off the land and wrote up that experience so it could be transmitted to the flyers and other people in the Navy. Toward the end of the war, the Craigheads were just about to take off and do the same thing on an uninhabited island close to Japanese islands for a similar purpose. After World War II was over, the Air Force hired them as civilians to consult with them on their survival course. They made a fine contribution.

Part of the academic curriculum included "Recognition." I say this with some family pride because one of my brothers, Howard, who was a dean at Ohio State University worked on the academic curriculum of our Pre-Flight Schools. He worked under Frank Ward, Navy commander, and later a great admiral. Frank Ward told him, "We have to teach recognition." Howard said, "How do you teach it?" Ward replied, "We use the British system, the WEFT system, which has a slang synonym of "wrong every time." So Howard wondered about how he'd teach recognition. He knew of the work of the psychologist named Sam Renshaw at Ohio State University who had developed a new method of teaching eye training and memory. San Renshaw was asked to apply that system to recognition. It was the system installed at all our pre-flights, that later was adopted for all Navy training of all ships and aircraft. The Army, Air Force adopted it, then Great Britain and all of our allies took it over. Quite an international feat for the Renshaw system which resulted from the application thought of by my brother, Howard.

Q: Isn't that wonderful, that's justifiable -

Adm. H.: That's right.

Q: Of course, when you speak about recognition, it's recognition of everything, not just the plane.

Adm. H.: Oh, yes, ships, planes, tanks, vehicles.

Q: Land, everything.

Adm. H.: And rapid reading is part of it, too.

Q: Oh, is that so, that's interesting. That would have been in the early days of rapid reading.

Adm. H.: It was one of the first experiments and the Navy at Pensacola has used rapid reading training since that time.

Q: I want to get some of the sort of basic things of this as to where was this training going on?

Adm. H.: Admiral Radford's program had several sides to it. He wanted to recruit and interest all the people he could get who were physically qualified to fly. So, we organized coaches recruiting teams and sent them all over the country.

Q: This was the first group you got?

Hamilton #1 - 56

Adm. H.: Some of the first group of coaches we got. For instance, Bernie Bierman was the head coach from the University of Minnesota and he had Bud Wilkinson, George Sauer as part of his recruiting team in the Mid-West.

Q: So you actually got the initial group to get the other people into the program.

Adm. H.: That's right.

Q: Did you put them on active duty and grade or did they make them part of the military?

Adm. H.: We were able to indoctrinate the first group at the Naval Academy. The Naval Academy opened rooms for us. We had four courses of one month's duration each for 200 officers, so we trained 800, indoctrinated them almost immediately. I think we started in February or March and we indoctrinated 800 officers. Then part of them were sent out to recruit cadets and other officers and some went to four pre-flight schools which were all designed to take about 1,800 cadets and give them a fourteen week training course in athletics and academics -

Q: How did they come out of the Academy, as ensigns?

Hamilton #1 - 57

Adm. H.: In rank accordance to their age and experience.

Q: I see.

Adm. H.: They got commissions like other reserve officers.

Q: Like I did, for example.

Adm. H.: Yes. We commissioned nobody over lieutenant commander.

Q: I see. And then they went out and they got, what, men who came in as enlisted or as pre-flight to become aviators. How did they take them into the pre-flight schools?

Adm. H.: Well, our specialized recruiting team embarked with the regular naval recruiting service to get cadets. They were so successful in signing up 80,000 cadets. Then the Army told Admiral Radford, "The Navy either has to release these people as civilians to be drafted, or put them in uniform." So, Admiral Radford started a lot of additional schools. I think there were sixteen Pre-flight schools. There were War Training Service Schools; I think there were thirty-two of those. These WTS schools were another type of flying school around civilian air fields.

We assigned these officers and coaches to those schools, to run these programs, and cadets were put in uniform, and given a syllabus of training which all fitted in with the general plan.

They went to WTS school and Pre-Flight Schools. Pre-flight school. Then to primary flight training bases at such Naval Air Stations as Hutchinson, Kansas and Olathe, Kansas and Los Alamitos, California, et cetera. There were sixteen of these primary flight bases and the cadets got their initial flight instruction there. If they passed primary training, they went to intermediate flight training at Pensacola, and Corpus Christi Air Station. If they passed Intermediate, the cadets went on to advanced flight training which was held at Jacksonville and Miami Air Stations.

Q: I think that at the end of Side One of the tape we were talking about the set-up which you established for aviation training at the beginning of World War II. I have the feeling that what you were doing was something completely new for the Navy and setting up a complete organization of the little corps and then the expansion and then the complete integration into the overall Navy. Am I judging that correctly?

Adm. H.: Perhaps it came out piece-meal and I'll try to

repeat and go over this again. Actually, I probably described my division or portion of the organization which Admiral Radford put together for aviation training under Admiral Towers and the Bureau of Aeronautics. It was all integrated as a part of the naval aviation system and Admiral Radford had the courage of lengthening out that training period in order to turn out perfectly trained pilots and crewmen to do the job that he envisioned. My part, in addition to the Pre-Flight Schools, was to put together the physical training of the whole structure of naval aviation which not only included the training bases, but also ships and tenders and bases where operating forces were working.

The first job right after Pearl Harbor was to obtain the instructors, whom we got from coaches and professors of physical education and academics, take them to the Naval Academy for indoctrination training and to work out the syllabus of training for the system. Also, we recruited a cadre of Naval Academy graduates who were in civilian life and not currently connected with the Navy. The Bureau of Navigation said there weren't any available that we could get. I asked if we could be assigned all I could find, and they agreed. By letters and telephone calls and using the Naval Academy directory we found a lot of them and they were all anxious to serve. We were very successful, but when we got to one hundred graduates, the

Bureau of Navigation cut us off. We were fortunate to have this very group of graduates who came in and took administrative roles and places in the academic ranks, and modeled our pre-flight schools on the Naval Academy training.

The four original pre-flight schools were established at the University of North Carolina, Chapel Hill; University of Georgia, Athens, Georgia; University of Iowa at Iowa City; and St. Mary's College at Moraga, California. Several of us went out to select these sites and we had quite an interesting time doing that.

For instance, we recommended that the Navy buy St. Mary's College which was in financial trouble at that time. The Navy elected to rent it, but later on we needed expansion and put another pre-flight school at Delmonte, California. The Navy did buy this beautiful hotel site and later converted it into the post-graduate school which it still uses very beneficially there. It was a good buy and so would have been St. Mary's.

Q: Which St. Mary's?

Adm. H.: The school at Moraga, California.

Each of those pre-flight schools capacity was about 1,800 to 2,400 cadets. A new group of 200 came in every two weeks and graduated fourteen weeks later. Some of the first athletic instructors were coaches used to recruit

Hamilton #1 - 61

athletes. They were sent out with the Navy recruiting teams to recruit cadets and people like Bernie Bierman, Bud Wilkinson, Matty Bell, people who were popular figures did attract youngsters, and we got some 80,000 cadets signed up. We got so many that Admiral Radford had to install other schools, prep flights, war training service schools to put the cadets in uniform, and all these cadets were usefully employed in preparatory work to their flight training.

Q: Was this because their actual flight training didn't have room for this many?

Adm. H.: That's right. From pre-flight schools, the cadets went to the primary training bases and there were sixteen of those. The cadets learned their first steps in flying at the Primary bases and continued their physical and academic training. From Primary they went to Intermediate training which was at Pensacola and Corpus Christi, and having graduated from there, the cadets went to advanced training at Jacksonville and Miami. Receiving their wings, they then were ordered to operating squadrons and incorporated into the squadron organization.

Q: How many would you say you handled all the time in the time that you were there? How many did you run through the program?

Adm. H.: There were 80,000 cadets.

Q: You said 80,000 - somewhere I had picked up a figure 250,000.

Adm. H.: No, I don't think so. I believe that was the extent of the pilot training. Now, of course, there were the air crew men training, done at Memphis training center and Norman, Oklahoma; Jacksonville, and there were lots of other bases like the gunnery training at Clinton, Oklahoma, and the school which were training officers and men for Escort carriers, the CVEs that were being built and the crews were formed in Tacoma, Washington - also near Portland, Astoria. Our athletic instructors were made part of the training and instructor personnel at those schools.

Q: I understood that you felt strongly that the men at the head of these four schools were such outstanding people.

Adm. H.: I want to emphasize how lucky we were to get outstanding leaders as commanding officers of the first four pre-flight schools. We got Scrappy Kessing as captain and commanding officer at Chapel Hill, North Carolina; captain Hanrihan at Iowa City; Captain Chip Smith at Athens, Georgia; and Captain George W. Steel at St. Mary's in California. These were outstanding retired officers who came on active duty and were just superb in administering those schools.

Assisted by the Naval Academy cadre plus these coaches and professors, we had great people to run it - corresponding to a conviction of mine, if you have good people, you have a good program.

Q: Oh, yes, I certainly agree with that. What puzzles me is the fact that you, as the aviation branch, were able to get these people out of civilian life, and I would wonder if you ran into conflict at any point with BuPers and some of their people.

Adm. H.: I would say we had cooperation, but we also had some difficulties along the way. I think we ruffled their feathers quite a bit and they ruffled ours some, but in the main, we got along pretty well. One amusing story, I think, that is pertinent is when I was sent out to Detroit to make the presentation to football coaches. When I got back and was ordered over to Admiral Radford's staff, I understood that Lieutenant Commander Gene Tunney, the heavyweight boxing champ, was disturbed by my presentation.

Hamilton #1 - 64

I'd never met him but he was in charge of the physical training program of the Navy at large. So I called and made a date with him to go over and have a cup of coffee and talk it out. We went down to the cafeteria and got our coffee and I said, "I understand that you were disturbed by my making this presentation for the program that Admiral Radford wants to install in naval aviation, and I think that's needless." He said, "as a matter of fact, I was disturbed. I just can't conceive of the Navy putting their training program in the hands of a bunch of fat and drunken football coaches."

Q: Dear me. Did he know you had been a coach?

Adm. H.: Yes, he knew I had been a coach. That kind of raised my ire so I replied as soon as I could, "Well, I guess you don't understand the whole concept is to use competitive sports in the training of these young pilots. The greatest competitive teachers that I know of in the country are the football coaches and I think they can do a better job than a bunch of punch-drunk boxers."

Of course, that was the start of a beautiful friendship. Actually, we have both mellowed a great deal and I've seen him since, so we get along all right, but there is another amusing story about him. We found that he was interested in some of the same applicants who applied to us. We had interviewed them and gotten their papers in

Washington. So, he came in one day and was looking over some of those. "Dub" Bayliss, who was a naval flyer, temporarily with us because he had migraine headaches and was grounded, got in a conversation with Gene Tunney. Dub tried to emphasize our use of competitive sports. Tunney replied to him in the following, which I repeated at a breakfast which Scrappy Kessing gave for Jack Dempsey and his manager. So, I was quoting Dub Bayliss, quoting Gene Tunney; Tunney said, "Well, if I were to fly in combat with some pilot from a carrier, I'd much prefer not to fly with one who'd been up drinking coffee and cursing in the wardroom, but would rather fly with a pilot who'd been in his room reading Keats and Shelley." Whereupon Dempsey's manager Max Waxman said, "Keats and Shelley, who'd dem bums fight!"

Q: It's a good story.

Adm. H.: There were lots of funny incidents along the way. Another one which was quite historic, at least to me, was the day I had a call from Admiral Radford. He wanted me to go over to the White House and see Mr. Harry Hopkins. Mr. Hopkins' son was contemplating going into the service and wanted to know about naval aviation, so I was to go over and explain the program. I went over, and sat outside Mr. Hopkins' office for quite some time. He was tied up in some crisis that came up, so the time ran on. About noon somebody came out and said, "Well, Mr. Hopkins still is involved and can't see you. Would you wait and while you are waiting, would you like to have luncheon with Mrs. Roosevelt?" Naturally, I said, "I think that would be very fine" and accepted very readily. I was led up to the second floor and introduced to Mrs. Roosevelt, who had a lady guest who was a newspaper columnist.

We had a very delightful luncheon and I found that she was a most charming person. Although I had never found her very good looking, I somehow forgot it when I looked in her eyes and she just acted herself. Anyway, I was certainly taken by her and her presence and personality. Toward the end of the luncheon she said, "Well, young man, what are you doing?" I explained briefly what it was and she said, "Have you any problems that you haven't been able to solve?" I sort of wondered whether I should mention anything but I bit the bullet and said, "Yes, as a matter of fact, there is." We had been struggling to establish football schedules with all the colleges in the country for our pre-flight schools, as well as the Army and Air Force service teams. The colleges had very kindly adjusted all their schedules to include us so we had top schedules.

It was a continuation of our conviction that physical

training and competitive sports events should be emphasized and kept going during the war years at all the high schools and colleges. Commander Tunney advocated cutting out all these schedules to save transportation during war time. The War Transportation Board was issuing rules prohibiting transportation use for sporting purposes. I explained this to Mrs. Roosevelt and said this would damage our concept of keeping physical training going in the United States. Well, a week later an executive order signed by Franklin D. Roosevelt cleared all of the athletic schedules from the restriction. It was a very notable thing in my mind to have that lovely lady go to bat for us, so to speak.

Q: I think she was a great lady.

Adm. H.: I guess I've rambled on here but I do want to say that we got the greatest cooperation from the officials at all these universities at North Carolina, St. Mary's, Georgia, and Iowa and those relationships were very helpful as our schools started to operate. They cooperated so well, and helped us in what we were doing.

Q: I recall the fact that there was a naval recognition school set up at Ohio State University. Is that the same thing you described that your brother did?

Adm. H.: That was set up as a result of Sam Renshaw's adaptation of his techniques for recognition and he trained the instructors in naval recognition at Ohio State in that school. The Navy did recognize, finally, Sam Renshaw's work, and Admiral Artie Doyle went out there to a wonderful dinner to pay honor to San Renshaw. It was quite a nice occasion which I attended.

Q: But on Side 1 you describe your brother amplifying that and that's what this refers to, doesn't it?

Adm. H.: That's right.

Q: Now let me see, do you think we need to cover any other - one question I meant to ask, how long was the actual training once they got into the pre-flight, until they got to be aviator?

Adm. H.: Actually, it ran about fourteen months.

Q: Fourteen months.

Adm. H.: It was fourteen weeks at pre-flight. Then they went on, but the whole training program went on about fourteen months.

Q: I see. Well, I think you have pretty well covered that. Do you feel there is anything more you want to add before we go on? I do know that you received the Legion of Merit which I think we should mention.

Adm. H.: Yes, both Frank Wickhorst and I received the Legion of Merit for the work we did at the pre-flight schools, and a number of our officers were decorated for this work.

Q: And were you - what grade were you at that time? Lieutenant commander?

Adm. H.: Yes, at that time, I was lieutenant commander. This came right after the war started.

Q: We haven't talked much about your personal life in all this time.

Adm. H.: I want to go over one other point, too. We did some experimenting that I think is interesting. The Harvard laboratories, Dr. Broohau, had a series of physical tests, which were first a "pack test," and this was changed into a "step test," where they tested the physical degree of fitness of each individual through the cardio-vascular system recovery. Naval Aviation kept records on every one of these cadets at each stage. Also, there was a course in relaxation, not given to all of them, but some experimental classes in relaxation were set up under a Dr. Fahey. I talked to many of these guinea-pig individuals later and they said that they had found it very useful in recovering from hard flights and fatigue. They could apply the principles of this relaxation course and be able to sleep and relax very readily. They thought it was a good course. We had other tests to test the reaction time of a cadet in hundreds of seconds; how soon a cadet would see a light, the periphery of his vision, and to test not only how wide his vision was, but also how fast he reacted to different combinations of lights flashing in various sectors. These were valuable tests and showed that the reaction time of a cadet could be improved by the training in various sports.

Q: I think it's interesting here also to put in the note that your syllabus for this school is available and it's going to be made part of the package.

Adm. H.: I have the original syllabus, both for physical training and academic work which I'll be happy to forward with this and have it stored where it is available if they ever want it. Also, the Naval Institute, after World War II, printed the text books which our instructors had written. These manuals were an enlargement on these syllabi, and for years they were the best textbooks in all eleven sports that were available. They were sold to colleges and high school professors throughout the country by the Naval Institute.

Q: That's interesting.

Adm. H.: Also the book on survival written by the Craighead twins was outstanding. I think I have not mentioned that at the pre-flight schools, each cadet spent about 4½ hours a day in some kind of activity in physical sports instruction or competition. Many people think that's a lot, but those cadets certainly were in top shape and turned out to be superb aviators. At the end of the war the Navy Department sent out four psychologists to interview flyers. They went out to all the aircraft squadrons of all types, and asked individuals in confidence, "Name two pilots you'd rather fly with in combat than any other two in your squadron, and name two you'd rather not fly with." The doctors took those names. Then the doctor went back through all the records of the individuals named in both categories, and made an analysis of it. I have a copy of that report which I'll be glad to give to you.

Q: I think it would be fascinating. Did it prove anything about whether the particular type of training was good or bad?

Adm. H.: They did prove that the ones who had the highest marks and the highest participation in sports in the preflights were predominant in those pilots they preferred to fly with, and the ones who weren't desired as flying partners had relatively poor marks.

Q: I see. I think that would be a very interesting report.

Adm. H.: Yes, and I know there are lots of exceptions to that. Some very good flyers I've known have had very little interest in sports.

Q: Is that right?

Adm. H.: But this was a study that was made at the end of the war, and it seemed to prove out, in part at least, that the program was successful.

I have elaborated on the pre-flight part and I think I should mention the other part of the contribution of these V-5 officers in operational squadrons and carriers and tenders and bases, after serving at the pre-flight schools and other bases. Most of them got into combat units and were useful in many, many ways in all kinds of jobs as well as in athletic assignments. We had eight of these officers aboard the Enterprise while I was aboard and they did all sorts of jobs. Captain Felix Stump, who was then a captain aboard the Lexington, told me that one of the best officers aboard was "Nerky" Moseley, who was assistant gunnery officer. I'm very proud of this group. I think it's a great documentary to the resourcefulness, the versatility of the coaching profession that they can go into jobs that they know nothing about, and produce effectively without having too many books or pictures drawn for them on how to do it. They just get the job done.

Q: It is a tribute they're making and it's intended, of course.

Adm. H.: Yes, and I'd like to say that has been a proven, a fine documentary for that group.

Q: Now, up to this time, you'd been able to, at least since the war time, to be with your family pretty much.

Adm. H.: That's true. I don't think I have mentioned that I did get married along the way, in 1932. I was very lucky to win Emmie Spalding from Coronado whose father was pastor of Christ Episcopal Church there. We've had two fine sons and they have grown into manhood, so we're enjoying a good family life. I learned early to push Emmie in the door first and generally found that she made friends and created a situation where people would accept me too, and we've had a great relationship. She's been a great asset.

Q: Well, in my observation only in the short time I've seen you, I should think it's mutual.

Adm. H.: We have a fine thing going, and I would say that anything I've done, she has certainly been a part and parcel of it. I think there's that old cliche that behind every successful man, there stands a very surprised mother-in-law.

Q: That's right, that's one of them. The other is a wife who keeps saying, no, no, don't do it. Well, I think we might get to a little bit of your activities, or at least begin on your activities when you went overseas after the assignment as operations officer. That actually - assistant operations officer lasted up until when you went to BuAir and that lasted until June, 1943 and then it was June, 1943 that you went overseas.

Adm. H.: Admiral Radford had told me that he would release me when the schools were underway - so, I got away May of 1943 and was ordered to the Big E, the _Enterprise_, which I joined in Pearl Harbor in May of 1943 and that was a stroke of luck, too. I really feel that that ship is the champion of them all, and I was most fortunate to be ordered to her.

Shortly after I joined her she went back to Bremerton for needed overhaul. We were in Bremerton until October of '43 getting new saddletanks for our gas fuel system and new radar. She needed refurbishing because she'd taken a beating in her earlier operations, and parts of the ship were still blown out from bomb damage that had not been repaired. It was a needed overhaul and it gave time to replace about 60% or more of the crew. These veterans were given leave and assigned to new construction. We got large replacements of new people to join with a cadre of old-timers. We left Bremerton in October of '43 -

Q: You were there then, what, almost a year? How long were you in Bremerton?

Adm. H.: About three months.

Q: Three months, yes. Strangely enough it was a coincidence I was there then and I remember the _Enterprise_ in the shipyard.

Adm. H.: Is that right? Well, the Big E had already made a tremendous record, but to me it was one of the most remarkable things that the old crew - and personnel was changing all the time - would pass on their "know-how" and their pride to the new crew members coming on, and they would carry on in that same fashion. We had minor trouble getting shaken down for a while, but then returned to efficient operations. If the Essex class carriers which were bigger, would carry more planes, the Enterprise was determined to carry the same number of planes in their air group. This necessitated the Enterprise developing the catapulting of planes for the initial launch. The Big E did not have the side deck elevators nor did we have the space that the Essex class carriers had.

Q: Do you want to specify what your job was and who the CO was before we continue on?

Adm. H.: I'm glad you brought that up. Captain Ginder was the captain of the ship when I first joined her and John Crommelin was exec and they truly were great officers. John Crommelin in particular left a heritage of great things in naval aviation. He was one of the best stunt pilots I've ever seen, and he had great ability, too. He had his own way of doing things which was sometimes hard to follow, because it might not be exactly standard with other carrier's operations. So, we had to adjust them some, to operate the same way other carriers did. But we always felt that his legacies permitted us to do carrier operations a little better.

We had a great group of officers aboard. Walt Chewning was in charge of our catapults and arresting gear, and I think he was mostly responsible for developing the technique that we had in catapulting the early planes of our launches. Since then catapulting has become standard in all the carriers, but <u>Enterprise</u> made the first widespread use of it. I was air officer at that time. The first war operations we went out in were the raids on the Gilberts and Marshalls. Then we had Air group six aboard with Butch O'Hare as the air group commander with Fighting Two in it. It was in those raids that we had the misfortune of losing Butch O'Hare, who was a congressional Medal of Honor winner for his previous action when he was aboard the <u>Lexington</u>. He shot down five planes in one pass over a Japanese squadron. During our raid on the Marshalls the <u>Lexington</u> was hit by a torpedo from a Jap night torpedo squadron. The next night we expected to be under attack again, and Butch O'Hare with the torpedo squadron skipper, Phillips, worked out a technique where we would launch O'Hare and Philipps in a torpedo plane which had a radar on its wing. We vectored them to the lamplighter, the Japanese plane that came up to trail us and to light with parachute flares the area for an attack.

Butch and Phillips catapulted in the dark and flew to a position astern of this plane and Phillips, with his radar, then directed O'Hare to close in on it, and we saw the Jap plane flame up as Butch shot him down in full sight of our task force. Then, after Butch was ordered to vector around and rejoin the torpedo plane, I heard Butch say, "Oh, I'm hit." It's believed there was poor communication in a torpedo plane and the gunner of the torpedo plane opened up on Butch as he tried to rejoin. I called to Butch to keep talking so we could get bearings on him, but he didn't answer. We searched for a couple of days and never did find him. That's a sad, sad story, but I always get a thrill out of going into O'Hare Airport which they named after a great hero and a great guy.

This episode was really the beginning of Navy night fighting in the Pacific as a result of O'Hare and Phillips' work. Bat teams were formed of a division of fighters and they had radar in their wings. They served on all the carriers as night combat air patrols around the carriers, and it was really Butch's work which initiated this. Also, the next operation that the Enterprise went on, we picked up a Bat team along with Air Group 10 which had been left on Maui to continue their training while we first went out with Air Group 6.

Bill Martin, who was squadron commander of the torpedo

planes was especially visionary in his training. He trained his torpedo pilots in night attacks with torpedoes and low level bombing and developed their skills in this way. He also fitted two of his torpedo planes with extra belly tanks which fitted into the bomb bays of the TBF. Air Group 10 came aboard and operated from the _Enterprise_ for a long period of time and started in with the attacks on the Marshall occupations where four ships were damaged and twelve planes were destroyed. The next raid was on the impregnable Japanese base of Truk. Our task group got in with surprise and was very successful in attacking this major base. In the Truk attack ten Japanese ships were sunk, twenty-eight damaged, and seventy-five planes destroyed. Part of the ships destroyed and damaged were the result of a night masthead level bombing attack delivered by Bill Martin's torpedo squadron with the training he had given them, and this was continuation of an emphasis on night operations.

Q: How did you relate to those operations?

Adm. H.: Well, I was in charge of planning the operations from the ship. The staff of the admiral made the direct plans, but then we had to coordinate those plans and we participated with the air group commanders to figure out how we would carry out the mission on the ship and also away from the ship.

Q: I want to relate it to you personally.

Adm. H.: Well, I was involved. There are so many. As I said before, an aircraft carrier is such a great team of air plot, CIC, fighter director officers, flight deck crews, hangar deck crews, aviation maintenance, bombing supply details, electronics, radio - all of them work so closely together. It's a marvelous team and the air officer has the coordination of those different facets or elements aboard ship.

I wanted to point out the continuation of interest in this night operations which eventually at the end of the war, the <u>Enterprise</u> was the first night carrier and I'll cover that a little later. But, this raid on Truk was led by Killer Kane, the Fighter skipper, and the bombing squadron commander was Commander Dick Poor and Bill Martin with the torpedo planes and Roscoe Newman was the air group commander at that time.

Air Group 10 hit Jaluit on the way back from that raid. The next operation was a raid on Palau, Woleai, and Yap where our Air Group 10 went in and made raids. But the Japs had apparently gotten the word and removed most of their ships before we hit. After that operation we went back to Majuro Lagoon where the ships would replenish and get ready for the next operation without going back to Pearl. A week later the Enterprise was in Task Group 58.3 in support of the capture of the Hollandia area on the coast of New Guinea. The Enterprise here accounted for 81 Japanese aircraft destroyed. On the 29th and 30th of April the group raided Truk and the Enterprise damaged five ships and destroyed twenty-three planes. On the 1st of June the Enterprise returned to Majuro Lagoon. On the 6th of June the ship got underway with Task Force 58 under Admiral Spruance and on 11 June, she launched her planes against Saipan Island. The Marianas occupation was to last until 5 July and the Enterprise share in the destruction of Japanese forces in the area amounted to three ships sunk, two damaged and thirty-nine planes destroyed. Fourteen Jap planes were shot down at dusk on 15 June when the ship repelled a torpedo plane attack. On 19 and 20 June occurred the battle of Philippine Sea in which Enterprise damaged three enemy ships and destroyed thirty-two enemy planes.

In addition, it was Enterprise's search plane that located the Japanese fleet when it looked as if it had escaped. There again, it was Bill Martin's torpedo planes with the extra fuel tanks, and they were able to extend the search and keep track of the Japanese fleet which was trying to get away.

Q: Can you expand on this and your relationship? Is this when it became the turkey shoot operation?

Adm. H.: That is right. During the Battle of Philippine Sea the Jap carriers and force were detected by submarines heading for Saipan where for some time the invasion of Saipan had been taking place. So, Task Force 58 went part way to meet this Japanese force and the Japs launched most of their carrier aircraft to make an attack on the American force. Admiral Spruance, by history at least, indicated that he had a responsibility to defend the forces invading Saipan, so he did not proceed headlong to try to intercept the Jap fleet. He stayed in proximity of Guam and Saipan, to not only hit the Jap fleet if he could, but to remain as an interdiction force for our invasion forces.

Almost all our planes were launched as combat air patrol to take on the invading Japanese air strike, and that is what is called the turkey shoot because our fighters shot them down in great, great numbers. Then the Japanese planes were ordered to go on to Japanese fields on Guam for landing and refueling before going back to their carriers. Our planes followed them over to Guam, shot them down as they were trying to land and our bombers and torpedo planes bombed the Jap fields on Guam. It wiped out the Japanese air groups.

Our task force was so occupied with those attacks that

we took some time to deliver a bombing attack against the Japanese fleet. Finally late in the afternoon, Admiral Mitscher launched a strike which was led by Killer Kane, our *Enterprise* air group commander. This strike from all our carriers hit the Jap fleet late in the afternoon and was quite effective. They sank several ships and did a lot of damage and it was when they were coming home, our planes - which were critically low on fuel - that Admiral Mitscher ordered all the ships to light up and use search lights to try to attract the returning planes as quickly as he could, and they would land on any carrier they could get to before they ran out of gas. *Enterprise* had forty planes in that strike and I was talking to Killer Kane who was in the downwind base leg on the carrier approach when he ran out of fuel coming up to the ramp and went into the water. We had fifteen planes out of our group go in the water with nineteen people, and the destroyers and escorts were plying back and forth picking up downed pilots in the night, all the ships with their lights on. The carriers were moving back and forth also.

It was finally decided by Admiral Reeves and I believe Captain Gardner to convince Admiral Mitscher and Admiral Spruance to leave the destroyers to this task and for the carriers to get on with following the Jap fleet and see if we could hit them again in the morning. So about midnight the carriers were detached with escorts and they left a number of destroyers to search for downed pilots. Bill Martin's search planes did locate the Jap fleet the next morning, but they were out of range and the Jap fleet got away.

Q: How many of your people were lost, if any?

Adm. H.: We had nineteen people in the water and before we left we had reports that eighteen were picked up. We had only one missing and that was Killer Kane. Then we spent three or four days chasing that Jap fleet.

Q: Excuse me, was he ever located?

Adm. H.: I'm going to get to that.

Q: I'm sorry. I got too anxious.

Adm. H.: We were about three or four days on this pursuit of the Jap fleet. When we came back in that area we came in company with these destroyers that had been left there to search. We received the blinking searchlight signal, "We'll trade one flyer for twenty gallons of ice cream!" The word was passed on the Big E. You never saw such elation on a ship and when Killer came over on the high line from the destroyer back to the <u>Enterprise</u>, I have never seen such an expression of love of a whole ship of men for one individual as was evident at that time.

Q: That's wonderful, isn't it?

Adm. H.: Yes, it was a great thing.

Q: Very touching.

Adm. H.: Killer was quite a guy and everybody was so happy to have him back.

Q: That's wonderful.

Adm. H.: So that's a vivid memory of that turkey shoot that you spoke about and it was a great victory. The Japs never replaced the experienced pilots that they lost at Midway, and also in this battle, so that was a very decisive thing. I think that it was a great victory.

Q: In our opinion, what would have happened to those pilots, what would have been the loss of life if Admiral Mitscher hadn't made the decision to have all the lights on?

Adm. H.: Well, we would certainly have had more planes

go in, and ditch in unlighted areas of the sea, and they would not have been concentrated in one area around the carriers where they were readily picked up.

Q: Because some did make the carriers?

Adm. H.: That's right and it was - oh, yes, many of them did. That decision, I think, saved many planes, many lives. One interesting fact is that we had one Jap plane, the red ball on his wing, came right over the flight deck and apparently he was looking for a place to sit down too, rather than trying to dive into the deck like some of the kamikazes did later.

Q: What happened to him, did he -

Adm. H.: I don't know, he just went off probably and ditched.

Q: He didn't land!

Adm. H.: He did not land on our carriers.

Q: It would have been a wonderful story if he had landed! I have a recollection from history that there was one battle, and I'm wondering if this is it when Admiral

Spruance did, in effect, withdraw rather than pursue as some people thought would have been a better maneuver. Do you have an opinion on that?

Adm. H.: I do, I think Admiral Spruance was a terrific leader and naval officer and I have read everything about him, a marvelous man. He was of a different nature from Admiral Halsey and I think many aboard the force were disappointed that we did not take more aggressive action in trying to hit the Jap fleet then. However, he did have the responsibility of protecting that invasion force. It's like grandstand quarterbacks on Monday morning, they always know better how to coach. But, I think the Naval War College did the same thing to Admiral Halsey at the Battle of Leyte Gulf which we'll come to later, but I don't think they treated Admiral Halsey as understandingly as Admiral Spruance in this case.

Q: Where was Admiral Halsey at this point?

Adm. H.: He was not with the force; they would assign the ships and make it Task Group 58 and then Admiral Spruance would operate it. For about three months Admiral Halsey with his staff would come in, we'd become Task Group Force 38 and that staff would have prepared the operation orders and be all ready for the next set of operations.

Hamilton #1 - 88

Q: So this was the alternate force at the time of the Philippine Sea?

Adm. H.: That's right.

Q: But you were always there.

Adm. H.: The ships were the same, they just changed the numbers of the Task Force.

Q: Now at what point did you become exec, have we gotten to that yet? I think that was a little later. Were you still air officer during the Gilberts and Marshalls?

Adm. H.: It was about in there. I don't have the exact date. Cecil Gill was exec, later was detached, and I became exec.

Q: I indicated that that would have been about June of '44, would that be correct?

Adm. H.: I think that that's probably -

Q: That you were air officer for a year and then exec from about June of '44 through the end of the Leyte Gulf operation.

Hamilton #1 - 89

Adm. H.: Yes, I think that's right.

Q: Shall we continue on, I guess we were up to the Philippine Sea, right?

Adm. H.: Yes, we just had that discussion and then there was the raid on the Bonin Islands and occupation of Palau. The aircraft carrier task group supported that, and the landing forces found very stiff opposition ashore at Palau. There was a lot of action trying to bomb and attack shore installations in that operation.

Then came raids on Nansei Shoto and raids on Formosa which was to try to beat down the Jap plane forces before the occupation at Leyte Gulf, so those raids took place prior to the action off Leyte Island. Of course, the battle of Leyte Gulf was quite a spectacular one with the three Japanese forces coming in Surigao Strait and San Bernadino Strait and the northern force off Luzon. <u>Enterprise</u> was in the southern task group and in the meantime, we had had Air Group 20 come aboard and they were another fine air group led by Dan Smith as air group commander. Air Group 20 had Fred Bakutis as commander of the fighters; Emmett Rierra with the bombers and Sam Prickett with the torpedo planes. They were a very aggressive, excellent air group and did untold damage to the Japs. Commander Fred Bakutis in our first strike in the early morning spotted the

Japanese force coming up Surigao Strait and attacked that group and reported them. Fred Bakutis was shot down by antiaircraft fire and was able to get out of his plane in his rubber boat. He was in the water about a day and he was surprised to have a submarine come up almost under him and pick him up. One of our submarines had those reports, picked him up, and he eventually returned to the ship about two months later having gone back to Australia on the submarine and then being transported back from there.

Q: Miracles now and then happen, didn't they?

Adm. H.: That's right. While this flight was in the air, Admiral McCain then was operating under Admiral Halsey in charge of the task groups. He ordered all three of the aircraft task groups to concentrate on the force coming up San Bernadino Strait, and there were many attacks on those ships. I have a photo of torpedoes from our Air Group 20 hitting the Musashi which was the great Japanese battleship. She was sunk at that time after taking a lot of hits and damage.

Q: Let's take that photograph and label it number one because that's the first one we've described.

Adm. H.: All right, I will. These attacks went on during

the day, and of course, our U.S. northern task group was under attack from Jap navy planes and the Princeton was sunk. The Essex was under heavy attack all day. These Jap air attacks were quite a threat. So, that night I was on the bridge with Captain Glover who was then in command. He had relieved Captain Gardner who had had the ship for quite some time. I think I failed to mention it.

Q: He was between Ginder and -

Adm. H.: That's right. Captain Gardner was a brilliant, officer and very experienced aviator as was Captain Glover, so we had some great skippers. The last report was about 9:30 at night that the Jap force at San Bernadino Strait had turned back. We had no flag aboard the Enterprise then but we had the flag circuits aboard ship so Captain Glover shared that information with me that night. We applauded Admiral Halsey's decision to attack the northern force where the planes which had sunk the Princeton and attacked the Essex, were quite a threat to our force. He'd decided to go after them about 9:30 that night after the above report. Admiral Halsey has been criticized a great deal because in hindsight he probably should have left the battleships striking group to protect the strait, but he went after the northern force and the next day demolished - he sank four carriers up there and a lot of other ships. Of course, the San Bernadino Japanese force did turn back that night and delivered a very devastating attack on the jeep carriers who were supporting our Leyte landings. Admiral Halsey did come back and practically demolished the whole Jap fleet before they could get back to Manila. I think it was regrettable that the ships had to be attacked, but I'm a firm believer that Admiral Halsey is the greatest naval officer of any navy of all time. This criticism of him is like criticizing the half-back for carrying the ball in the wrong arm when he runs over the goal line for a touchdown.

It has generated quite a lot of controversy which I think has been unfair to Admiral Halsey's image, and I regret very much that Admiral Halsey did not have as good a writer to write his biography as Admiral Nimitz did in Professor Potter. Admiral Nimitz' book was superb as was the one on Admiral Spruance, so being such a Halsey fan, I regret we don't have a little more laudatory book about him.

Q: You knew him personally, of course?

Adm. H.: Yes. He had command of the Reina Mercedes when I was a midshipman and he was officer in charge of the boxing team, and he was an inspirational leader at that time, along with some other great leaders at the Naval Academy at that period. We had Captain Doug Howard who was a former Navy football coach and head of the Ordnance department and we had Scrappy Kessing there, along with Admiral Jonas Ingram and Bill Ingram, and the leadership of those men, I think, made a great difference certainly in our football results of the year 1926.

Q: I was wondering if you were in any contact with Admiral Halsey after this situation of the Leyte Gulf going north situation to know how - did he know about the criticism at the time? Do you know how he reacted to it, how it affected him?

Adm. H.: Oh, yes. My wife, Emmie, went to school with his daughter, Margaret, and they were close friends and Admiral Halsey always expressed a great interest in Emmie everytime, asking about her when I would see him. After he lived in New York, they tried to have the Big E made into a shrine, a museum, at Washington, D. C. Congress passed a law to permit this but Admiral Halsey became ill at that time and none of the rest of us were able to raise the money without him to bring about that desirable aim of having the Big E as a naval museum in Washington.

Q: Well, was he devastated by the criticism or did he

let it roll off him, or are you aware?

Adm. H.: I think he had a very phlegmatic attitude toward it. I think he felt he had done his best and he was willing to let sleeping dogs lie. As a matter of fact, he showed a great amount of interest in trying to help wherever he could in any public cause. I think he gave a lot of himself during that period when he was quite ill.

Q: Were you aware of the message that came through which became so famous?

Adm. H.: Yes.

Q: Were you aware of it as it came in?

Adm. H.: We got that message, yes, and we -

Q: Maybe we ought to quote what the message is in case someone forty years from now wonders what we're talking about.

Adm. H.: Well, it was a message from Admiral Nimitz saying, "All the world wants to know where you are," on the basis of Admiral Kinkaid's question of the threat of the Japanese force and it was - but as I say, hindsight, you do a lot better with it. At the time, Captain Glover and I were on the bridge; we read the same information that Admiral Halsey was getting. We applauded his move to go after the northern force.

Q: What did you think about that message when it came in?

Adm. H.: Well, it was a shock and I guess we were hoping that our force could get back in time to get the Japanese force.

Q: So, to put on the record that for that period you did receive the Bronze Star with a combat V and a citation for the particular operation in the battle of Leyte Gulf.

Adm. H.: Well, I'm happy that I got a decoration out of it, but all the duties were so much the same in all the operations that I can't figure out any special reason I got the Bronze Star and was also awarded the Legion of Merit with a combat designation on it later, but it was all the same kind of operations which were involved with the ships' activities, so the whole ship was involved in them. There wasn't anything very individual about it. I think that -

Q: But every man had to be there to do his job.

Hamilton #1 - 96

Adm. H.: Oh, yes. Well, I had a great thrill when I was detached from the ship a couple of days before Christmas at Pearl in 1944. The crew of the ship presented me with the United States Ensign which had flown from the main truck, the <u>Enterprise</u>, October 24 and 25 at the battle of Leyte Gulf. I prize that as a great, great treasure and I will see if one of the museums doesn't want this flag because I think it belongs there and not in my box.

Q: Am I correct in understanding you have offered it to the Naval Avaition museum?

Adm. H.: No, I have got to do something about it.

Q: You haven't done that yet?

Adm. H.: I haven't done anything about it, but I think it belongs, you know, as a relic of the ship.

Q: Oh, definitely.

Adm. H.: So, that is too valuable to be resting in my care.

Q: How did your duties shift from air officer to exec?

Adm. H.: Well, for a time I carried both jobs for about

a week or two, until Dick Poor was designated as air officer. I kind of eased into one from the other and, of course, had been aboard ship for some time so becoming exec was not such a great change.

I do have one story that might be interesting. Admiral Black Jack Reeves was aboard a great deal of the time and was a wonderful flag officer. Everybody respected him greatly and you tried to do your job or you heard from him. We had a very irrepressible, young guy named Jerry Flynn who had been a cheerleader at Notre Dame and was an Irishman with a lot of spirit. He was our recognition officer trained in the Sam Renshaw system, and he was in charge of the lookouts up at the flag bridge. One day Admiral Reeves said, "Mr. Flynn, what kind of a plane is that out on the horizon," and Ensign Flynn said, "Admiral it looks like a B-25 to me, Sir." The admiral said, "Well, it looks more like a B-26 to me," so Jerry says, "Well, admiral, I'll bet a week of my salary against a week of yours." The admiral didn't like that very much, so he wrote a letter to Captain Gardner and asked that Mr. Flynn be put in his room for a couple of days to think things over.

It became my lot from Captain Gardner to deliver the message to Flynn, so we put him in his room and he was there for a couple of days, but soon was back on duty, doing a good job. He ran the ship's radio station and had a gossip column every night and was good humored and kept the ship's company in good humor. A little while later, the ship had a smoker when we were in Ulithi Harbor, and a happy hour with boxing bouts and the band playing and all that, and Jerry Flynn, of course, was master of ceremonies. So, all the sailors were grouped around the elevator which served as a stage and they were all packed in the hangar deck and hanging, really from the rafters. Flynn said, "Well, I guess you know why we're here tonight," and the sailors all cheered. He said, "We've all come to say goodbye to Admiral Reeves," and he said, "You know, I want to tell you a story. I had the same battle station as Admiral Reeves." He said, "One day Admiral Reeves said to me, 'Mr. Flynn, this ship isn't big enough for the two of us,'" and Jerry then said, "We're mighty sorry to see Admiral Reeves leave tomorrow."

Admiral Reeves practically fell off his chair he laughed so hard. It was kind of a good story, I thought.

Q: It is a good story. I wanted to ask you if you could describe Ulithi from your eyes, the harbor there.

Adm. H.: It was a beautiful atoll with quite a large expanse of water, but the magnificent thing about it was the assemblage of ships. One just couldn't believe that we had that many ships operating, and they all came in there and they got their supplies and replenishments and their rest. Again, here was Scrappy Kessing in charge of that base and he, interestingly enough, had an island called Mog Mog where one of our V-5 wrestling coaches, Charlie Speidel of Penn State was in charge. The ships would send their men over there for beer and baseball, a little recreation before they came back to the ships. Typically, Scrappy Kessing gave the Enterprise a lot of transportation so we got all our men over every day for the time we were in there. I would try to send over to his mess a crate of oranges or ice cream, or things that we had that he probably didn't have ashore, but he would always pass them on to the base hospital there.

So, I'm a great admirer of Scrappy Kessing. He did this tremendous job for Admiral Halsey and the whole Navy in operating these advanced bases at Tulagi, then Bougainville, then Ulithi and finally he had the base at Yokosuka. A great achievement for him and rare contribution to the success of the war effort. Scrappy Kessing broke the mold as did Admiral Halsey!

I think I'd like to go back and mention that probably the greatest honor that ever happened to me, happened during this time. The ship was in Eniwetok harbor and Captain Gardner made admiral and got dispatch orders to depart right away. At the same time, Bureau orders came in from Washington ordering me in command of the Enterprise, so I had the great honor of commanding that ship. We steamed out of Eniwetok and went back to Pearl to get a new propeller on the ship. I had command of the ship for a short time until Captain Cato Glover came out and relieved me of command of the ship. We went back and joined the fleet again at Eniwetok and away we went again. So, that is the greatest break that a commander in the Navy, I think, ever got, so I'm very proud to mention that.

Q: Being a commanding officer - there is nothing like it, is there?

Adm. H.: That is right, and of that ship Enterprise at that time, I think that was very significant.

Q: What would that have been covering, a period of two months?

Adm. H.: It was about a month.

Q: About a month. That was wonderful. Now then are we coming to the end of your duty -

Adm. H.: I think I missed this - I mentioned that about the leadership and vision of Bill Martin in his advance work in night flying. He came back as air group commander of Air Group 90 which was a night group, and Admiral Gardiner returned to the Enterprise with his flag to operate at night from the Enterprise. This took place in the latter stages of the war. In addition to the ship operating planes through the day, they maintained flights of interdiction and attacks at night over Japan, Okinawa and other spots in different actions. I think the work of Admiral Gardner and Bill Martin in this connection, and of course, Captain Bud Hall, was skipper of the Enterprise during that time, a very competent and wonderful officer was outstanding.

Q: This may be footnote rather than addenda. There is a book, The Big E, the story of the USS Enterprise, Commander Edward P. Stafford, USN, with a forward by Admiral Radford, in print. It is a big book and it is a fine book for anyone who wants to pursue the detailed story of the Enterprise. It was printed in 1962.

Adm. H.: I operated as exec again until about the end of November when we had raids on the Philippine Islands and Formosa and Okinawa. We were involved in those. Then we went back to Pearl, and I was detached as exec, and ordered as training officer at ComAirPac which was located at Pearl Harbor, under Admiral Towers. Later Admiral Montgomery relieved him as ComAirPac. This was a very interesting job. It involved my flying from Pearl to the many bases around the Hawaiian Islands where we had air groups in training to go aboard carriers and to be deployed forward. It was my responsibility to inspect and observe them and certify them for duty aboard carriers, and to be deployed into the war zone. It gave me a chance to fly with a lot of wonderful people and observe their ability. Truly they were good. We were getting the results of the excellent naval aviation training and these same young cadets that started off in Pre-Flight were out flying now and they were very good.

Part of the responsibility was to administer the replacement pilot pool which was called Air Group 99 in Pearl, Air Group 100 on the West Coast. There three new pilots would be teamed up with one experienced pilot and they would be available when carriers lost planes and pilots. A four plane division would fly the replacement planes aboard at a carriers' request. The attack carrier always lost more planes than pilots, fortunately, so the carriers' skippers were a little spoiled. They would ask for say, four fighter planes and four bombers, then these replacement pilots who would be on a jeep replacement carrier would fly the new planes aboard and be delighted to join the group and find a home for themselves. Often the skipper of the attack carrier would pick off the division leader and send the three inexperienced people back to the replacement carrier, for further transfer to the pool on Saipan Island. The replacement pilots morale was going down. I was able to get Admiral Montgomery to put out an order that if an attack carrier took four planes, they took four pilots. When they did that once and they saw that the inexperienced pilots were just as good as the others, we had no problem, and morale went up as all of the replacement pilots found a home. Then if the attack carriers needed a plane, they took the pilots readily, illustrating how effective the training system was which Admiral Radford established.

Q: Now, you've been referring to replacements of pilots and so on, did you have anything to do with the actual training back at Pearl before they left Pearl or were they -

Adm. H.: Oh, yes, we would order air groups to run training exercises aboard carriers that were there for practice work. The Air Groups also conducted attacks on every Navy ship that came in the Hawaiian area. Each was subjected to simulated night attack and other aircraft attacks, and then the ships would get towed sleeves where they could fire their antiaircraft guns. All this was part of the training exercises which I was responsible for with that job. We scheduled all that and had the air groups working against ships and training on rocket ranges. We had shore target areas with simulated revetments and oil tanks as the normal targets started to change from ships to attacking air bases and also shore base defenses.

Q: And, of course, new techniques were constantly coming out as new planes were developed, I would assume.

Adm. H.: That's right, new planes and all the jeep carriers were coming out from construction and CVLs. Some had observing squadrons that spotted aircraft fire for shore bombardments.

Interview #2 with Rear Admiral Thomas James Hamilton, USN
(Retired)

Place: 7580 Caminato, La Jolla, California

Date: April 22, 1978

Subject: Biography

By: E. B. Kitchen, Commander, USN

Q: I think we cut off a word at the end of that other tape.

Adm. H.: We were talking about air groups with fighter planes which observed gunfire for ships which took place in the battles in Okinawa and Iwo Jima. They were very effective in those operations.

I think I should mention, too, that ComAirPac also had advanced headquarters on Guam after Admiral Nimitz moved CinCPac out there. Admiral Gunther was ComAirPac forward operating out of Guam. This facilitated training also on the air fields out there.

During the time that I was training officer at ComAirPac, the Japanese war ended. VJ Day came and of course we were all delighted. Shortly after that I was ordered in command of a jeep carrier the Savo Island, CVE-78. We were given the assignment of operating in the Magic

Carpet operation which was returning Army troops home, and we made trips from Okinawa back to the States with Army troops. It was a good experience to have command of that fine little carrier.

We were in Seattle when I got word from Admiral Fitch, the Superintendent at the Naval Academy, that he wanted me back there and I was ordered back to the Naval Academy and operated there through the seasons of 1946 and 1947 as head football coach. This was a tough experience because we were a little out-manned in those years. All civilian colleges had returnees from GIs that represented five or six classes of athletic talent. They also has some experience in the service, and some of these same coaches who had been in pre-flights, took a lot of those players back to the colleges with them. But, the Naval Academy had a group of stars playing during the war, such as Hoernshmeyer and Minisi and Clyde Scott and Ellsworth, and Bob Kelly. The Navy allowed them to resign if they did not want to continue at the Naval Academy. West Point allowed no resignations and they retained their stars who were outstanding - Blanchard, Davis, Tucker, Poole, that group. The Navy football teams had a difficult time as far as wins and losses, but I have never been associated with football squads, or with young men, who were as valiant and courageous as the group we had there then. They would take a loss and come back the next week all the stronger. My admiration certainly goes out to them. We had such people as Leon Bramlett as the captain of the '46 team and Dick Scott, captain of the '47 team, Pistol Pete Williams, Hawkins Shimshak, Bobbie Schoefferman, Tex Lawrence, Markel, Newbold Smith, Bob Hunt, Dick Emerson, et al. They're a great group of people, and they kept coming stronger all the time.

In the first season we won one and lost eight, and we played Army a team with Blanchard and Davis who had not lost a game for 39, I think, games. We had them on their knees. We lost the game 21 to 18 in Philadelphia, but Navy was on the two yard line when time ran out. Chewning made a long run at the end of the game and we had missed conversions after touchdown, so the score was 21 to 18 at the time. Chewning made this run to the two yard line and with a minute and 32 seconds left, Navy got only three plays off in that time. The confusion - the crowd ran out on the field. They pulled all the guards to guard President Truman who left the game early and there was no protection of the field, so the crowd went out on the field. The noise and confusion slowed the action as the team could not hear in their huddle. The time ran out before we could get our fourth play off and it's been a nightmare to me ever since, because our Navy team deserved to win and they had Army on their knees at that time. It was a heartbreaking loss, but you have to live with it.

In '47 we had a little better season, but not much. We were still faced with the same odds, trying to play Notre Dame and all the other colleges with their returned people, and Navy still with only three classes including plebes. As I say, we weren't too successful but it was an episode in my life of gaining admiration for a wonderful group of young men who refused to quit in the true Navy tradition.

I then became athletic director, and George Sauer who served aboard the Enterprise with me, came in as football coach. At this time they were putting ships in mothballs and it looked as if I would be going to school for the rest of my life. I had some feelings that having had all this work in physical training, the challenge that our schools should accept in maintaining fitness of youth, I felt, I guess, a lack of resistance to several offers that came to me to work in this field, physical education and athletics. So, I gave it a great deal of thought and with the prospect of, as I say, ships being in mothballs, not many jobs open, I accepted the challenge to go to the University of Pittsburgh which I did in 1949. I was there for ten years as athletic director, working in this field. It's a fine institution and I had the opportunity not only of planning, but raising funds to build needed facilities for the university in the form of a gymnasium and playing fields, swimming pool, et cetera.

During this time, we twice had casualties with our football coaches, so I took over and coached in 1951 and 1954 at the University of Pittsburgh. It was in 1954 that I even had to coach against the Navy. Red Dawson, our coach, had a heart attack on Tuesday before the Navy game. Pittsburgh had lost by large scores to USC, to Minnesota and Notre Dame prior to the Navy game. So with that situation, I took over as head coach with the prospect of meeting Navy and Eddy Erdelatz' "team of desire" at the Pitt stadium. It was a marvelous game and I have never had the experience again of being so proud of both teams on the field as I did in the closing minutes of that game when Pitt won 21 to 19. Both teams played such wonderful, hard-hitting football that I was proud of both teams. Navy went on to win at the Sugar Bowl that year. It was the only game they lost, but Pitt went on successfully. We lost to Ohio State which was ranked as national champion that year. We beat Nebraska and West Virginia and Pitt had a good season.

That again took me back to my old love of football. During those years at Pitt, I was active in the NCAA. I was appointed the first chairman of their TV committee in 1950 when TV was just coming on the scene. There was a lot of debate and concern about what the competition of TV would do to attendance at football games. All the colleges rely on the income that comes from football game receipts, so we ran quite a study. There were some schools, Notre Dame and Pennsylvania, principally, who wanted to corner the whole TV market. The philosophy of our committee was that the loss from TV on gate receipts should be spread and diminished as much as possible. We devised a plan to try to have many schools on a schedule provide excellent football contests, but to limit the number of appearances that one school could have on TV.

The first contract we sold for $1 million. Now you can see how it has changed. I think the present contract runs something like $16½ million for TV. If a team gets income from TV, why should not that school feel the effects of competition as well as the TV competition they are causing at other schools. That has been the philosophy ever since. They've weakened the appearance rules a great deal. I think too much. They've probably given ABC too much leaway in directing the schedules, but overall it's been a successful operation and a very interesting one for TV.

During this period, I was also chairman of the NCAA committee on fitness for about six or seven years. I was appointed by President Eisenhower and President Kennedy, to their advisory committee on fitness. We saw the Council on Physical Fitness established in Washington, and a modest program has developed, and it has been ably administered, by Bud Wilkinson and now Casey Conrad.

Also, during this time I spent sixteen years on the U.S. Olympic committee and served on their executive board from 1948 to 1964. It was very interesting duty but frustrated by the politics that go on in the Olympic organization. I was chairman of the Olympic development committee which we urged be established to try to provide and develop better U.S. teams in some of the sports where the United States was not well prepared. In part of this movement we were able to get a women's advisory committee established for the Olympics. This group, with our backing, conducted clinics for six different women's sports. I think this has been instrumental and helpful in the development of women's sports which now is moving ahead rapidly in the colleges and high schools. Regarding the U.S. Olympic Committe, the colleges and high schools provide the programs, the coaching, the equipment, facilities, but the competent coaches don't have enough say in the Olympic organization. I hope that this controversy will be solved and the United States can have cooperation from all its resource organizations which are infinitely superior to any other nation in the world. No other country has athletic systems that compare with our school and college programs in the United States. If we can just mobilize all the resources we have, the U.S. continues its world leadership in the Olympics and sports.

Congress is now considering legislation to assist

the Olympic movement, and if they can affect a reorganization in the Olympic Committee, then it can improve.

The colleges have been pretty steadfast in their determination to try to improve the situation. They found they could not do so from within the Olympic organization, so they dropped out.

Q: But you've had some national awards. Would you mention them?

Adm. H.: I guess I'd better cover the period on the West Coast. I left the University of Pittsburgh, in 1959, the Pacific 8 conference was formed, and I was asked to come out as commissioner. I served for twelve years as commissioner of the Pacific 8 conference which included the eight top universities on the West Coast. This was a very interesting job, administering the conference activities and athletics of these eight schools. It involved administration of the Rose Bowl game where we have a contract with the Big Ten conference. We take some satisfaction that since 1959 Pac 8 won thirteen out of nineteen games with the Big 10 in the Rose Bowl. Prior to 1960, the results were pretty much one-sided the other way.

The Pac 8 conference wins from five to seven national championships a year, which no other conference has done.

Our conference has super teams in these institutions in baseball and tennis and track, swimming and gymnastics. We have won five football championships. Johnny Wooden, who incidentally was a V5 officer during the war, set a record for all achievements winning nine out of ten national championships in basketball at UCLA. So, those were very interesting years, continuing my interest in sports and in fitness. During this time I served on the NCAA committee on drug abuse and also was appointed to Governor Reagan's committee in California on this subject.

This was very instructive to me listening to the doctors on Governor Reagan's committee talking about the epidemic that was hitting our youth. I believe the NCAA has been fairly effective in its work. It enlisted the coaches of most sports to work against drug abuse, and they have carried on a campaign against the use of drugs for youth on all the NCAA TV sports programs. The NCAA issued posters for all the gymnasiums of high schools and colleges, and they have distributed about 11 million pamphlets a year on this subject.

The commissioners of all the conferences in the country have a good organization. I was president of that body for a term, and enjoyed my contacts with these other conferences very much.

I retired from the Pacific 8 in 1971 and have returned to southern California, to La Jolla, with my wife Emmie, and we are delighted to be visited occasionally by our sons. Bill has a lovely wife, Lili Beth and they've given us two lovely, little granddaughters. They've been here recently, so we've enjoyed them. There are fifty-five of my class of '27 who are retired around here in the San Diego area, so we meet every month for a luncheon and have a very good time.

I guess I should mention that in 1965, I was greatly honored by being inducted into the Football Hall of Fame at their great dinner in New York. Then in 1970 the Football Foundation honored me with their gold medal award. I think it was an award recognizing the contribution of the Navy's sports program in keeping sports alive during the war. In making me the recipient, they were honoring not only the Navy, but all the many coaches who came in and worked in the Navy. This was certainly very much appreciated.

The National Association of Athletic Directors honored me with their Jim Corbett award which is an award they give each year to one athletic director. The NCAA in 1975 awarded me their Teddy Roosevelt award which is an annual award, a very great honor. Another recognition along the way was when the Football Writer's Association named me "Football man of the year" in 1942. I was chairman of the United Fund Drive in Pittsburgh while I was there. I've had a lot of interesting assignments which have added to my career and satisfaction.

I think I would be remiss if I didn't acknowledge with thanks the receipt of the Jim Lynah award from the Eastern Collegiate Athletic Conference. Also, the Touchdown Club of New York honored me in 1945 as their football man of the year. There's also an assignment I had on the NCAA football rules committee for six years which was a very pleasant and interesting job in working on the football rules. This is a fine body of men and I'd like to point out here that Captain Paul Dashiell, "Skinny Paul Dashiell," a chemistry professor at the Naval Academy served on the football rules committee longer than Walter Camp did, for 27 years. He was one of the few men responsible for the forward pass. When President Teddy Roosevelt insisted that rules changes be made -

Q: Teddy Roosevelt?

Adm. H.: To reduce the injuries taking place about 1905, Paul Dashiell was one of those who instituted the forward pass. While I was coaching at the Academy we visited with Captain Dashiell very often, a delightful man. I tried to persuade him to write a book about all his memories of the game. He used to referee the games between Princeton and Harvard, and Yale and Harvard, in a derby hat with a cane. He had pictures to show it. He had so many interesting memories of the game in its early stages, and of course, the history of Navy football. The first coach at the Naval Academy was John Reeves, who later had such a great career in the Navy and was commander in chief of the U.S. fleet about 1930.

Q: Was that Blackjack's father?

Adm. H.: No, this is John Reeves with the goatee beard. Other Naval Academy graduates who were head coaches were Captain Berrian, Captain Doug Howard, Captain Dashiell, Jonas Ingram. They all coached the Naval Academy team. A very interesting group of people have held that job and they later became a part of naval history. All were great naval officers.

I had some recommendations which I thought probably I would indicate. I think I mentioned before that I think that the Navy should study whether a more active, all-embracing physical program in athletics and recreation would be a useful move in maintaining interests, morale, and help in recruiting in this peacetime Navy. It would add a great deal to the pride and morale aboard ship, I believe.

I've always felt that the Navy does not make enough use of its retired personnel. The idea was once offered of having selected groups of people, retirees in various areas, be assigned advisory responsibilities preparing position papers and policy on various countries. It's my understanding that they have small sections in OpNav of, say, a captain and a commander and maybe a couple of junior officers to keep position reports of intelligence on various countries as it relates to Navy policy and United States policy. Say, they took the San Francisco area when Admiral Nimitz was there, using his great knowledge and the knowledge of other very, competent, retired people there, they could have assigned, say, China or Russia to a San Francisco group and give them the intelligence and let them write out their policy recommendations, which could be considered along with the more active recommendations of the groups back in OpNav.

Q: Well, Admiral Sharp, for example, who went through all the Vietnamese thing and who did Korea; but any one of those people it seems must make their contribution after retirement through a civilian organization or the Navy League. I think it's a marvelous idea. Have you written it out; have you made a proposal?

Adm. H.: I haven't written it out, but I know it was presented to BuPers. I just wanted to comment that I've seen this vast amount of talent represented by various people available such as Admiral Sharp and Jimmy Thach and Cliff Cooper. There ought to be some way to utilize them.

Q: To use that talent. I couldn't agree more, even me!

Adm. H.: Yes, you could name them all along the line, Dutch Deuterman and all of them - they've all had vast experience. This would give an outlet and be useful, so that's a thought.

Q: I hate waste and I hate waste of brains more than anything else.

Adm. H.: I do hope that in the mobilization plans, if there's a large confrontation, that the Navy does remember what Admiral Radford did in naval aviation training. They have the pre-flight now at Pensacola, but I think they should remember that there's a very valuable group of people in the coaching ranks who can be tapped.

Q: On that topic, I'd like you to describe what it is you are giving me to ship to the Institute and what the Institute has which you know they publish that relate to this matter. Would you describe the three books there that I am going to ship?

Adm. H.: Yes, I have a book which is entitled, <u>United States Fleet Athletic Annual</u>, which was published about 1933 by Commander Andy McFall which reveals the extent of the athletic programs in the fleet at that time. I think this illustrates how an athletic program can be useful to the Navy in peacetime. Also, the two originals bound looseleaf syllabi for academics and physical training of the Pre-Flight schools are forwarded. This material was improved and copied in printed books which the Naval Institute published as text books for physical education. They gave the lesson plans that were carried on at various stations in the naval aviation program and I think are quite good. These were written by top coaches and revised for many years after the war was over, and the Naval Institute has copies of those, plus the survival book.

Q: Now the survival book was prepared by two brothers called Craighead and -

Adm. H.: They have that; I'm sure of it.

Q: I should say it differently. There were physical training manuals for eleven different sports published and distributed nationwide by the U.S. Naval Institute.

Adm. H.: Good, you said it better than I could.

Hamilton #2 - 120

Q: You told me that before. So, in any case, what we're saying is that these publications which the Institute knows and undoubtedly has, we are cross-referencing in this interview, so that anyone using this as a reference material would know where to go.

Adm. H.: That's right. I missed one little thing. I always have had great pleasure in taking part in sports. One of the sports I enjoyed so much in the Navy and outside of the Navy is squash. Any city where I would go, I found a wonderful group of men playing squash and this sport was a good entree into any city - where I met fine people I liked right away and developed good friends. Squash is a great sport for a quick workout. It's available on most naval stations and I hope the Navy continues to have courts, and keeps squash available for Navy people.

Q: What do you think of jogging?

Adm. H.: I think it's great, but I'd rather get my exercise playing some game.

Q: I see.

Adm. H.: Jogging is fine and has been proven to be an excellent conditioner. I think the Naval Academy athletic program is an excellent one. I hope we can maintain that. Captain Coppedge is an excellent choice as athletic director. I think it was a wise thing to continue the service of a naval officer as athletic director and retire him there. Previously, the two and three year spans of duty for incumbents did not provide the continuity that the job requires. By the time a person with a short term gets acquainted in the field, he goes to sea and you lose all his contacts. As in other areas, it's not only what you know, it's who you know.

Q: That's true.

Adm. H.: I think Captain Coppedge is having difficulty financing the vast athletic program that the Navy wants to continue. The Naval Academy is instituting women's sports now for the girl midshipmen and it's expensive. I think the Navy has to provide funds to keep this well balanced type of program going. The Navy, I think, has to do selective recruiting for the Naval Academy, and I think the coaches all realize that. It's my observation that they tend to over-concentrate on trying to select the blue chip athlete. Well, if you can get them, that's fine. But, the Navy isn't going to get as many blue chip athletes as some of the other colleges, so the Navy, I think, has to best use the system available to service academies. This system has some advantages over other colleges in that every midshipman has a scholarship. He not only gets his education paid for, but he gets paid for going to the Naval Academy. It's an excellent "deal" as athletes say in college. The opportunities for practice at the Naval Academy are superb. The coaching at Navy is tremendous. However, I believe with the small number of students enrolled at the Naval Academy as compared to the number at large universities, the Navy has to develop talent of its own. The Naval Academy in the past had JV teams with outside schedules; and plebe teams with outside schedules. The trend in collegiate athletics is to eliminate the freshman team and combine the JVs with the plebes and move some plebes into varsity competition right away. I think this hurts the development of needed individuals if you combine JV competition and plebe competition.

So my advice is to keep the program comprehensive and continuous from the NAPS program, the Naval Academy Preparatory School, and provide plebe teams, then JV teams to keep athletic development avilable for the limited number of athletic hopefuls the Navy gets, and try to bring out a star, say, in his last year. Our dedicated players who have worked their way up through the system and will be just as good as anybody if they continue to work over those years.

I think in conclusion I would like to say that I think

the Navy is the greatest organization that I have ever known. I think World War II was probably the greatest example of the magnificent cooperative effort of a nation's that the world has ever seen, and I hope the U.S. doesn't forget the lessons that we should have learned at that time. I appreciate the opportunity to make this tape and I hope that my remarks will be edited and refined a great deal.

Q: Well, your remarks are on tape and they'll come back to you just like you said it which really makes the human touch instead of making it a recital of a newspaper story or something of that nature.

Adm. H.: I'm sure there are a lot of errors and I hope they can be corrected.

Q: I think that the benefit of this program is that you have an opportunity to see it, of course, and if there are errors of fact, but the desire is not that you try to make it a finished, journalistic endeavor.

Adm. H.: Yes.

Q: The Institute, through me, thanks you for giving us your time.

As an addendum, Admiral Hamilton has some pictures

he's going to let me send, and I will identify them. I already identified number one which was the Japanese ship as it was being under attack from the _Enterprise_, and then I will list these others. Photograph number two is of the USS _Enterprise_ hit by a kamikaze pilot and shows the forward elevator blown 400 feet in the air. The caption is on the reverse side of the photograph. Photograph number three is also the _Enterprise_ with a near miss and lots of flack. Needless to say, there is a complete album of _Enterprise_ photographs, but they might not be as accessible as these three.

So, we are going to add another item to continue on with the _Enterprise_ feats.

APPENDIX

Report of Psychologists from BuPers of pilots in the Fleet toward end of the war.

BUMED-VX-AK
P2-5/A21

22 Mar 1946

WASHINGTON 25, D. C.

From: ChBuMed
To: CNO
Attn: Aviation Training Section

Subj: Cadet Physical Training Performance as Related to Combat Criteria Classification, report on

Refs: (a) CNO ltr, Op-35-G-WRK, Serial 287633 dtd 10 July 1945, BuM&S End. dtd 23 July 1945
(b) CNO ltr, Op-35-G-WRK, Serial 318633 dtd 4 Aug 1945

Encl: 1(HW) Subject report

1. By ref (a) CNO requested the combat criteria classification of Aviators who had been in the Pre-flight Training Program, for the purpose of correlating this classification with the achievements in the area of physical training. It was further requested that BuM&S assign a representative to assist in the analysis of this data.

2. By endorsement to ref (a), BuM&S suggested an alternate procedure. This procedure consisted of submitting a single alphabetical list of men for whom combat criteria ratings were available, and whose records showed that they had completed Pre-Flight School training. CNO was then to enter various physical performance grades on such a list and return to BuM&S for final computation of the predictive value of the various types of grades. A representative of CNO was to cooperate in the preparation of the final report.

3. By ref (b) CNO approved the alternative procedure and suggested that the single list of pilots classifications be forwarded, and authorized Lt. Comdr. Channell as a representative to cooperate with the representative from BuMed to complete the final report.

4. The final draft of this report is now completed and forwarded in compliance with procedures established in ref (a).

By direction of the Chief, BuMed:

J. C. ADAMS
Commodore (MC), USN

Enclosure (1)

CADET PHYSICAL TRAINING PERFORMANCE AT PRE-FLIGHT SCHOOLS
AS RELATED TO COMBAT CRITERIA CLASSIFICATION

Commander Ralph C. Channell, H(S), USNR
Lieutenant Charles L. Vaughn, H(S), USNR

I. INTRODUCTION

Late in 1944 BuMed assigned four H(S) Aviation Psychologists to the combat area of the Pacific for the purpose of obtaining evaluations of the combat performance of naval aviators. Some 10,000 evaluations on several thousand pilots were obtained as a result of this assignment. It was known that many of the men thus evaluated had been through the Navy's pre-flight physical training program. The present study was designed to determine whether there was any relationship between performance in the physical training program and subsequent evaluations of combat performance.

The basic and rather novel procedure used by the representatives of BuMed was to interview as many combat-experienced pilots as possible and to obtain from each of them the names of four pilots, two of whom they would like to fly with in combat and two of whom they would not like to fly with in combat. After the names were given, the respondents were asked to give reasons for their selections. This procedure has been termed the "nominating technique," and various reports of the work have been submitted to cognisant activities.

After the technique had gained rather general acceptance as a means of obtaining combat evaluations from the men who were actually doing the combat flying, CNO requested BuMed to furnish a list of names of the men chosen for the top and bottom groups so that records of their performance in the naval pre-flight training program could be pulled from the files and the men's accomplishments in training be studied.

A list of about 5000 names was provided by BuMed, and a search of the physical training records produced complete data on 1354 men, 707 of whom had been chosen one or more times for the LOW combat group, and 647 of whom had been nominated one or more times for the HIGH combat group. Since directives activating the project had specified that the designations of men as HIGH or LOW were to be held in the strictest confidence, the various physical training grades, measurements and indices were computed by CNO and submitted to BuMed for analysis in relation to the combat criterion. A representative of CNO served as consultant for this analysis.

II. ITEMS ANALYZED FROM PHYSICAL TRAINING RECORDS

After preliminary tabulations, the following items from the physical training records were selected for study in relation to the combat evaluations:

(1) Height of the men upon entering pre-flight school;
(2) Weight of the men upon entering pre-flight school;
(3) Stature index, viz.:

$$\frac{height}{\sqrt{weight}}$$

(4) Strength index, viz: $\frac{number\ of\ chins}{weight\ in\ lbs.}$
   (a) Upon entering pre-flight school;
   (b) Upon leaving pre-flight school;
(5) Composite test scores (based upon chins, pushups, jump-reach, speed agility, step test.):
   (a) Upon entering pre-flight school;
   (b) Upon leaving pre-flight school;
(6) Sports participation in high school and college before entering Navy:
   (a) Number of sports in which engaged to the extent of receiving a letter in high school or being on the varsity squad in college;
   (b) Participation or non-participation in each sport to the above specified extent;
(7) Composite grade on the Navy 4.0 scale in the physical training phases of the pre-flight program (composite based upon grades in sports - swimming, boxing, wrestling, soccer, football, hand-to-hand, gymnastics, military track - and composite test score)

Tabulations were made by place and time of entering pre-flight school, by naval rank when the respondents knew the men they evaluated, and by type of plane flown by the men chosen.

III. CHARACTERISTICS OF CRITERION GROUPS

Although in this study we were concerned primarily with differences between the HIGH and LOW groups in terms of the seven variables listed, a summary description of the population of men nominated is necessary for orientation. In brief the population of 1354 nominees for whom physical training records were available:

(1) Entered pre-flight school between April, 1942, and December, 1943, the most frequent entry date being February, 1943. (The average age of the men upon entering pre-flight school was 21½ years.)
(2) Attended the five U. S. Navy pre-flight schools open during this period in the proportions expected on the basis of the schools' total enrollments.

(3) Were principally Ensigns and Lieutenants (junior grade) when their colleagues observed their combat performance.
(4) For the most part, flew single-engine, carrier-type aircraft in combat, although a sizable group flew multi-engine planes.

Tables I through IV show this information in more detail.

Upon entering pre-flight school, the men:

(1) Ranged in height from 5'4" to 6'4", with an average of about 5'9½".
(2) Ranged in weight from 110 to 229 pounds, with an average of about 160 pounds.
(3) Were of medium athletic body build.
(4) Had participated in high school and college sports as follows:

17% in football	66% in no sports
15% in basketball	17% in one sport
7% in track	13% in two sports
18% in other sports	4% in three sports
	.2% in four or more sports

Norms on the strength index and physical fitness tests are not sufficiently well known to give ready meaning to these measures. However, they were distributed over a wide enough range to justify comparisons between the HIGH and LOW groups. Composite athletic grades, on the Navy 4.0 scale, showed a fairly normal distribution, except for an expected tendency to group themselves at the mid-points.

IV. RELATIONSHIP OF THE PHYSICAL TRAINING ITEMS TO THE COMBAT EVALUATIONS

Tables V through XII show the relationship of the seven variables to the combat criterion. These tables may be summarized thus (the statistically significant findings are underlined):

(1) Men who were eventually nominated in combat for the HIGH group tended to be somewhat taller when they entered pre-flight school than were men who were nominated for the LOW group. This difference was more pronounced in the multi-engine and unclassified groups.

(2) Weight on entering pre-flight school showed some, but not much, relationship to combat desirability. (Table VI).

(3) The stature index, as used in this study, was not significantly related to the combat evaluations. (Table VII).

(4) HIGHS tended to have a greater strength index than did LOWS, both when they entered and left pre-flight school. Breakdowns by pre-flight school attended revealed a consistent tendency in this direction for data from each school. (Table VIII).

(5) HIGHS tended to have a higher composite physical fitness test score than did LOWS (Table IX). Breakdowns by pre-flight school showed that the gross difference was largely a result of differences in scores for the Chapel Hill and Athens cases. This fact may reflect differences between schools in scoring, record keeping, etc.

(6) The HIGHS tended to participate in more sports in high school and college before they entered pre-flight school than did the LOWS. (Tables X and XI). There was no strong evidence in favor of any one particular sport as a superior prediction of combat desirability.

(7) The HIGHS tended to make better grades in athletics in the pre-flight schools than did the LOWS. This tendency was manifest in the data from each of the five schools: Of the various measures studied, this one gave the best differentiation between the HIGH and LOW groups. (Table XII).

As shown in Table III, the LOW group tended to have more Ensigns than did the HIGH group and the HIGH group more Lieutenants (junior grade) than did the LOW group, despite the fact that both groups entered pre-flight school at about the same time and with equal naval status. Differences in the length of time required to complete flight training are probably one factor. It is also known that the HIGHS tended to include officers of higher rank than the LOWS.

V. SUMMARY AND CONCLUSIONS

From the evidence in this report, the conclusion is indicated that the more desirable combat naval aviators in World War II (as nominated by their fellow pilots) tended to be taller, stronger, and more athletically inclined and physically fit than were the less desirable aviators. The more desirable combat aviators did significantly better in the physical training phases of the pre-flight program than did the men less desired in combat.

Studies can be made to determine the most efficient weighting and scoring of measures of sports participation, success in athletics, height, and strength, in order to improve present methods of selecting men for combat aviation duty.

The possibility that these same measures may be of value in selecting pilots for duty other than that of combat flying should be investigated.

TABLE I

DISTRIBUTION OF HIGH AND LOW GROUPS BY DATE OF

ENTERING PRE-FLIGHT SCHOOL

1354 combat nominees with phys. training records   11/45 RCC CLV

Quarter of Entering Pre-flight school	Frequency of Cases	
	HIGH Group	LOW Group
1942		
April - June	27	29
July - Sept.	82	68
Oct. - Dec.	128	154
1943		
Jan. - Mar.	188	207
April - June	141	154
July - Sept.	66	83
Oct. - Dec.	15	10
Date not know	——	2
TOTAL	647	707

Median and modal entry date   HIGHS --------- February, 1943
                               LOWS   --------- February, 1943

TABLE II

DISTRIBUTION OF HIGH AND LOW GROUPS BY PRE-FLIGHT SCHOOL ATTENDED

School	Frequency		
	HIGHS	LOWS	TOTAL
Chapel Hill	130	158	288
Athens	176	182	358
Iowa	140	183	323
St. Mary's	127	131	258
Del Monte	74	53	127
TOTAL	647	707	1354

TABLE III

DISTRIBUTION OF HIGH AND LOW GROUPS BY RANK WHEN RESPONDENTS KNEW NOMINEES

1354 nominees from combat groups   11/45   RCC CLV

Rank	Frequency		
	HIGHS	LOWS	TOTAL
Ensign	296	415	711
* Lt. (Junior grade)	337	278	615
* Lieutenant	12	11	23
Unknown	2	3	5
TOTAL	647	707	1354

* Breaking points for computing x^2

$$x^2 = 23.11$$
$$p << .01$$

TABLE IV

Distribution of HIGH and LOW Groups by Type of
Plane Flown at Time Respondents Knew Nominees

1354 Nominees from Combat Group		11/45	RCC CLV
	Frequency HIGHS		
TYPE OF PLANE FLOWN	HIGHS	LOWS	TOTAL
SINGLE ENGINE	425	424	849
MULTI-ENGINE	142	119	261
UNKNOWN	80	164	244
TOTAL	647	707	1354

Table V

Relation of Height Entering Pre-Flight School to Combat Criterion By Type of Plane Flown

From group of 1354 combat nominees with phys. train. records   11/45   RCC CIV

Height in Inches	Single Engine		Multi-Engine		Not Classified		TOTAL	
	HIGHS	LOWS	HIGHS	LOWS	HIGHS	LOWS	HIGHS	LOWS
64	1	2			1	3	2	5
65	14	14		5	3	6	17	25
66	17	29	4	5	3	18	24	52
*								
67	36	40	13	19	5	30	54	89
68	67	68	21	12	10	25	98	105
69	68	65	19	23	12	30	99	118
70	70	76	24	17	10	16	104	109
71	53	44	24	21	14	13	91	78
72	48	44	16	11	9	11	73	66
**								
73	32	18	8	6	3	5	43	29
74	13	10	8	1	9	5	30	16
75	5	10	5	1	1		11	11
76		3						3
Unknown					1	1	1	1
TOTAL	424	423	142	121	81	163	647	707

$x^2 = 4.45$ $x^2 = 13.01$ $x^2 = 2.03$ $x^2 = 25.80$
$n = 7$ $n = 7$ $n = 7$ $n = 7$
$p > .70$ $.10 > p > .05$ $p < .01$ $p << .01$

*Subjects above this point classed together for computing x^2; **Below this point classed together.

Table VI
Relation of Weight Entering Pre-Flight School to Combat Criterion By Type of Plane Flown

From group of 1354 combat nominees with phys. train. records 11/45 RCC CLV

Weight in Lbs.	Single Engine		Multi-Engine		Not Classified		TOTAL	
	HIGHS	LOWS	HIGHS	LOWS	HIGHS	LOWS	HIGHS	LOWS
110-19						1		1
120-29	11	14	3	7	1	5	15	26
130-39	57	51	15	16	9	18	81	85
140-49	80	102	18	25	18	38	116	165
150-59	97	107	38	26	14	37	149	170
160-69	85	61	29	20	14	25	128	106
170-79	60	49	16	19	13	18	89	86
180-89	24	22	14	7	7	10	45	39
190-99	6	8	8	3	1	6	15	17
200-09	3	2			1	4	4	6
210-19	1	3			2		3	3
220-29		1						1
Unknown					2	4	2	4
TOTAL	424	420	141	121	82	166	647	707

$\chi^2 = 9.52$ $\chi^2 = 8.33$ $\chi^2 = 2.20$ $\chi^2 = 13.55$
$n = 7$ $n = 5$ $n = 5$ $n = 8$
$.10 < P < .20$ $.10 < P < .20$ $.80 < P < .90$ $.10 > P > .05$

Table VII

Stature Indices of HIGH and LOW Groups
By Type of Plane Flown

From group of 1354 nominees with phys. train. records   11/45   RCC CLV

Stature Index	Single Engine		Multi-Engine		TOTAL	
	HIGHS	LOWS	HIGHS	LOWS	HIGHS	LOWS
13.5 +	50	66	18	21	68	87
13.0 – 13.4	177	160	53	39	230	199
12.5 – 12.9	146	139	51	48	197	187
— – 12.4	45	57	16	12	61	69
TOTAL	418	422	138	120	556	542

$x^2 = 4.62$ $x^2 = 2.41$ $x^2 = 5.14$
$n = 3$ $n = 3$ $n = 3$
$p \doteq .20$ $.30 < P < .50$ $.10 < P < .20$

Table VIII

Distributions of Strength Indices of HIGH and LOW Groups
Upon Entering and Leaving Pre-Flight School
By School Attended

From group of 1854 combat nominees with phys. train. records

STRENGTH INDEX	CHAPEL HILL Enter High	CHAPEL HILL Enter Low	CHAPEL HILL Leave High	CHAPEL HILL Leave Low	ATHENS Enter High	ATHENS Enter Low	ATHENS Leave High	ATHENS Leave Low	IOWA Enter High	IOWA Enter Low	IOWA Leave High	IOWA Leave Low	ST. MARY'S Enter High	ST. MARY'S Enter Low	ST. MARY'S Leave High	ST. MARY'S Leave Low	DEL. MONTE Enter High	DEL. MONTE Enter Low	DEL. MONTE Leave High	DEL. MONTE Leave Low
--24		5				6		1				1		3		1		2		1
25--29	8	45	1	1	1	16	1	1		14	1	5	8	9	1	1	4	4	1	1
30--34	21	45	9	25	7	42	11	25	4	64	18	20	5	44	3	4	8	8	2	8
35--39	61	64	40	50	57	71	58	76	29	81	40	67	21	45	8	44	23	26	11	14
40--44	51	33	48	55	80	35	64	49	59	53	52	61	49	28	23	49	49	17	55	22
45--49	8	7	22	26	51	18	51	22	51	7	33	22	23	7	35	7	34	9	35	7
50--54	1		4		18	3	7	5	12	2	5	1	19	1	54		4	1	18	2
55+			1		4	1	1		2				2	1	9	1	1	3	3	3
TOTAL	130	155	130	155	178	170	171	177	157	181	149	175	127	130	133	127	81	45	68	52
MEAN	37.5	33.5	41.7	39.7	39.7	36.3	40.1	37.2	37.5	33.5	40.5	39.4	38.5	35.9	42.5	41.5	39.2	36.7	43.5	40.1
$\chi^2 =$	3.96		2.61		4.55		14.20		3.61		5.51		12.07		4.10		7.76		8.82	
$p =$	<.05		<.20		<.05		<.01		<.20		<.20		<.01		<.05		<.01		<.01	

Total Entering Strength Index $\chi^2 = 36.00$, n = 1, P = .01
Total Leave Index $\chi^2 = 20.04$, n = 1, P = .01

Because of small n's, chi-square computed on basis of dichotomous classification. Interval of 34-35 was considered as the point of dichotomy for the entering test and the interval of 39-40 for the leaving test.

Table IX

Distributions of Composite Physical Fitness Test Scores of HIGH
and LOW Groups Upon Entering and Leaving Pre-Flight School
By School Attended

1884 combat nominees with phys. train. records

COMPOSITE TEST SCORE	CHAPEL HILL ENTER HIGH	CHAPEL HILL ENTER LOW	CHAPEL HILL LEAVE HIGH	CHAPEL HILL LEAVE LOW	ATHENS ENTER HIGH	ATHENS ENTER LOW	ATHENS LEAVE HIGH	ATHENS LEAVE LOW	IOWA ENTER HIGH	IOWA ENTER LOW	IOWA LEAVE HIGH	IOWA LEAVE LOW	ST. MARY'S ENTER HIGH	ST. MARY'S ENTER LOW	ST. MARY'S LEAVE HIGH	ST. MARY'S LEAVE LOW	DEL MONTE 11/45 ENTER HIGH	DEL MONTE ENTER LOW	DEL MONTE LEAVE HIGH	DEL MONTE LEAVE LOW	RCC CLV LEAVE HIGH	RCC CLV LEAVE LOW
10-14	1	1				2		3		2							1	2		1		
15-19	2	4				1		11		4		2		1							1	0
20-24	5	18		1		8		18		11	2	9	1	7	12	1	0	3	0	5		5
25-29	13	51	4	6	22	26	4	7	17	24	0	15	7	12	1	5	0	6	1	4	1	9
30-34	21	51	8	11	25	32	7	16	20	43	11	18	7	18	2	8	8	9	3	6	0	5
35-39	29	19	16	40	32	21	15	24	41	28	24	44	10	9	8	6	9	11	4	10	5	9
40-44	25	29	21	52	28	21	26	30	27	28	38	33	9	5	9	10	11	8	9	5	6	5
45-49	24	14	20	29	22	11	33	25	28	12	29	35	7	3	5	9	8	8	11	8	11	9
50-54	4	5	10	17	4	5	21	18	19	8	16	14	8	0	2	9	5	6	10	6	12	12
55-59	4	5	10	12	4	1	10	12	9	1	12	10	0	1	10	8	5	0	5	1	5	6
60-64			7	9			7	9	1		8	10	3		0	4	4	1	4		6	1
65-69			2	3		1	2	4	1		1	2	1		1			1	1		5	2
70-74											1	1									5	1
TOTAL	129	156	127	135	144	123	145	156	190	188	140	138	48	51	48	61	58	62	59	59

MEAN: 37.9 34.2 45.8 43.2 36.9 32.8 45.4 45.9 40.1 49.7 45.8 46.7 49.9 45.1 47.5

χ^2	13.15	8.19	10.20	6.69	.001	2.78	8.86	.019	.687	4.87
P =	<.01	<.01	<.01	<.01	>.98	<.10	<.10	>.80	<.50	<.05

Total entering composite test score $\chi^2 = 19.81$, n = 1, P = .01
Total leave composite test score $\chi^2 = 21.16$, n = 1, P = .01

Because of small n's in tails, dichotomous classification was used in computing chi-square. The interval of 34-35 was considered as the point of dichotomy for entering test and the interval of 39-40 for the leaving Pre-Flight test.

Table X
Participation of HIGH and LOW groups in High School and College Sports Before Entering Navy
By Individual Sport and Type of Plane Flown

From group of 1354 combat nominees with phys. train. records   11/45   RCC CLN

	Single Engine		Multi-Engine		TOTAL	
	HIGHS	LOWS	HIGHS	LOWS	HIGHS	LOWS
Football						
No. participating	87	71	23	9	110	80
No. not participating	329	347	115	109	444	456
Total	416	418	138	118	554	536
χ^2	2.00		5.17		4.31	
P	>.10		<.05		<.05	
Basketball						
No. participating	74	55	17	13	91	68
No. not participating	344	367	121	107	465	474
Total	418	422	138	120	556	542
χ^2	3.65		Insignificant		2.95	
P	<.10				<.10	
Track						
No. participating	38	32	7	4	45	36
No. not participating	378	400	131	116	509	516
Total	416	432	138	120	554	552
χ^2	1.00		Insignificant		.64	
P	>.30				>.30	
ALL OTHER SPORTS						
No. participating	81	74	25	16	106	90
No. not participating	337	348	113	104	450	452
Total	418	422	138	120	556	542
χ^2	.52		1.04		Insignificant	
P	>.30		>.30			

Table XI

Participation of HIGH and LOW Groups in High School and College Sports Before Entering Navy By No. of Sports Engaged In

From group of 1354 combat nominees with phys. train. records   11/45   RCC CLJ

No. of sports participated in	Frequency HIGHS	Frequency LOWS	TOTAL
0	396	493	889
1	118	107	225
2	101	78	179
3	30	26	56
4 or more	2	3	5
TOTAL	647	707	1354

* For computation of x^2, men below this point grouped together.

$$x^2 = 11.59$$
$$n = 4$$
$$p << .01$$

Table XII

Distributions of Composite Athletic Grades of HIGH and LOW Groups By Pre-flight School Attended

From group of 1354 nominees with phys. train. records   11/45   RCC CLV

Composite Ath. Grades	Chapel Hill HIGHS	Chapel Hill LOWS	Athens HIGHS	Athens LOWS	Iowa HIGHS	Iowa LOWS	St. Mary's HIGHS	St. Mary's LOWS	Del Monte HIGHS	Del Monte LOWS
23			1	5			1		1	
24			1	2	1		0		0	
25			5	7	0		0		1	
26			6	8	3	5	1	1	2	1
27			5	14	9	21	1	7	1	0
28		2	8	24	4	11	6	12	1	3
29	3	15	18	21	8	18	10	21	10	8
30	27	50	30	36	41	45	30	37	13	16
31	24	38	12	12	28	33	31	24	10	6
32	32	28	21	15	17	29	19	10	7	8
33	16	14	19	11	15	11	16	11	9	5
34	15	7	19	11	9	4	7	4	4	0
35	7	1	7	7	4	3	2	1	0	0
36	0	2	10	3	1	2	2	0	4	1
37	1		6	1				1	3	0
38			1	1					4	1
39			0	1					1	1
40			3						2	1
TOTAL	125	155	170	179	136	178	126	129	72	52
MEAN	3.188	3.106	3.154	2.980	3.086	3.024	3.103	3.027	3.175	3.073
$x^2 =$	15.40		23.47		8.07		11.72		10.68	
P =	<<.01		<<.01		<.02		<.01		<.01	

Original Plan for Pre-Flight Training presented by Tom Hamilton to Captain Radford. Dec. 1941

TENTATIVE PROPOSED

PHYSICAL TRAINING PROGRAM

for

NAVAL AVIATION

From: Head of Physical Training Department
To: Director of Aviation Training
Subject: Tentative Proposed Physical Training Program
           for Naval Aviation.

Enclosures:
   (A)   Tentative Organization Chart of Induction Center

1. In accordance with your directives and general plan, physical training is to be made an integral part of the flight training of pilots for Naval Aviation. This tentative plan is submitted on the subject, and the related matter of establishment of the Induction Centers, which form the keystone of the entire physical program.

2. The need for a physical program is very evident. Our pilots to be inducted into the Naval service in general come from a soft, luxurious, loose-thinking, lazy, peace-time life in our homes and schools, and must be prepared physically and mentally to meet and defeat pilots and personnel of our enemies who have been thoroughly trained in a purposeful and wartime physical and mental system for years; in fact, from childhood. Our athletic programs have developed mental alertness, agility, initiative and a sporting competitive spirit possibly superior to that of our enemies but there is little question that their youth are stronger, tougher, better physically trained and steeped in a nationalistic and fanatical frame of mind that drives them to carry out their ruthless methods of total warfare. No matter how mentally alert, agile, and clever an athlete may be in handball or other sports, he will be defeated invariably by an opponent only slightly less skillful and less imaginative, who has a great superiority in strength, endurance, and a cold-blooded will which pushes aside all rules to win. So in war!!! The mission then is to train our pilots not only so they are more skillful in flying technique and knowledge, but in one year and

subsequent training to place them on the field of combat stronger and tougher, both physically and mentally. To accomplish this, our methods must be revolutionary as compared with our peacetime life. And the most intensive, rigorous and comprehensive program of physical and mental training that the world has ever seen should be installed. Time is short.

3. The Induction Center is the whole foundation for this physical and mental training. The athletic facilities of very few of our educational institutions are adequate for the mass physical training of a large number of students. The schools taken over must have the necessary athletic plants. Most of these schools will be large and thus powerful in their opposition to being absorbed completely. It is most desirable that the entire college be taken over for it will detract greatly from the purpose, morale and benefits of our program if our Spartanlike life of discipline and hard work is paralleled by a modern college life on the same campus. The automobile and tire industries have been taken over by the Government due to war necessity. The need for adequately trained pilots is certainly no less important. During the last war the Universities were practically directed by SATC Commanders. The enrollment at all colleges will be greatly reduced anyhow, so a redistribution of the nation's educational facilities is in order for the training of youths for the life they must pursue.

4. It is recommended that four Induction Centers be established; one in each section of the country, namely: East, Middle West, South and West. Thus, with a total of 2500 students entering training each month at all centers, 625 would be inducted monthly at each of the four centers; with a three-months training, there would be 1875 students at each institution at all times. This number adapts itself better to the facilities of a number of schools, since very few schools have the athletic plant to accommodate 2500 students

if only these centers were established. It is felt that more than four would be "scattering the shot" too wide, as there would be difficulty in obtaining high grade instructor personnel, which is a large problem in itself for one base. Greater decentralization will produce wider variety in the quality of the product, and the cost would be greatly increased to take over the additional institutions and establish a basic service staff at each location. Four centers will give full sectional coverage. Until sites are investigated and a decision made from fuller knowledge, this program is made up on the basis of four centers.

5. The size and organization of each center are comparable to the Naval Academy, though of course the scope of the work is specialized and limited to the rapid turnover. The staff must be ample, and a recommended organization is submitted as Enclosure (A).

6. The routine of these establishments has been set up to prepare a candidate for flight training in the following basic fundamentals:

        1. Proper physical conditioning and strength.

        2. Knowledge of general naval lore.

        3. Knowledge of military drill and seamanship.

        4. Elementary training in communication and specialties.

To achieve these purposes within a three months preliminary training period, the daily routine below is proposed. The necessary instruction personnel and facilities required for this proposed plan are based upon the application of this training routine to the individual and to the total number of individuals enrolled at each Induction Center:

0500	Reveille
0510-0525	Setting-Up Exercises (Calisthenics or road work. Dip where water and weather permit.)
0550	Breakfast
	Clean up rooms, etc.

0700-0925 **First Period**

    Group A - Physical Drills

    Group B - Military Drills

    Group C - Academics

0940-1205 **Second Period**

    Group A - Academics

    Group B - Physical Drills

    Group C - Military Drills

1215-1225	Chapel
1235-1315	Lunch
1315-1345	Rest Period

1345-1610 **Third Period**

    Group A - Military Drills

    Group B - Academics

    Group C - Physical Drills

1615-1815	Varsity - Intramural - Voluntary Sports (compulsory participation)
1830	Supper Formation
1840	Supper
1930-2050	Study or Recreation (alternate nights.)
2100	Taps

NOTE:

        Group A -   Group inducted 1st month

        Group B -   "   "   2nd month

        Group C -   "   "   3rd month

The basic unit will be the platoon of 50 men.

The work is planned in each department to be progressive over the three months training, growing steadily more strenuous from the start to the finish. Each drill and academic period will be further divided into various subjects. The general breakdown and description of each activity follows:

(a)   <u>Setting-Up Exercises</u>

    0 -   15.   Calisthenics or Road Work.
                    Dip in water if practicable

(b)   <u>Physical Drills</u>

    0 -   25.   Body-building Exercises
   30 - 1:15.   Hard Labor - Woodchopping, Ditchdigging, etc.
 1:20 - 2:05   Drills in Selected Sports
 2:05 - 2:25   Cool off, Shower and Dress

(c)   <u>Military Drills</u>

    0 - 1:05   Infantry
 1:15 - 2:20   Military Arts Drills - Radio, Seamanship, Guns, etc.
                                Recognition, Parachute, etc.

(d)   <u>Academics</u>

    0 - :45   Lecture Course in Naval Lore
   50 - 1:35   Ground School Subjects - Mathematics, Aerology, Navigation,
 1:40 - 2:25   Study Period   etc.

(a) <u>Setting-Up Exercises</u>

Students will assemble outside (any weather) and take 15 minutes of calisthenics, consisting mostly of "tone-up" exercises to effect the circulatory system, to stretch muscles, and build up health and hardiness. Road work may be substituted for variety and, if water is available, the exercise should be followed by each man taking a quick dip or swim.

(b) <u>Physical Drills</u>

The 2 hour-25 minute period will be divided into four parts:

1. The first 25 minutes will be devoted to body building exercises, systematically working all the muscles of the body to ensure the harmonious development of the whole body. These exercises will increase in severity as the students progress in the course. These exercises will be conducted by the whole Battalion at the outset of the period.

2. The Battalion will be divided into two parts, two companies to take 45-minute drills in selected sports and the other two companies the 45-minute drill in hard physical labor such as woodchopping, land clearing, ditchdigging, etc. If no labor is available, mass games such as Push-ball will be employed. The two companies taking sports will be divided by platoons to the following sports for instruction and exercise:

        Boxing   Football
        Wrestling (Rough & Tumble)   Basketball
        Track   Military Sports,(Obstacle races, etc.)
        Swimming   Ju-Jitsu

The course in each sport will be comprehensive and progressive over the three months training as illustrated by a tentative program in Wrestling and Rough and Tumble, as follows:

WRESTLING - ROUGH AND TUMBLE

Training Period of 90 Days - 18 Drills

The Wrestling Rough and Tumble drills be taught in 3 General Divisions:

(A) Getting control of an opponent
(B) Rendering opponent helpless, or liquidate him
(C) Defense or escape from an attack

The first 30-day period be devoted to Division <u>A</u>, which includes the following six (6) drills:

(1) The Leg Tackle. Pick up and slam

(2) Arm Drag. Used to get behind and disarm an opponent

(3) Headlock and hiplock

(4) Front standing hammerlock

(5) Elbow blow under chin

(6) Scrotum blow

Second Period of 30 Days

Teach Division B - Render helpless

(1) Body Scissors

(2) Hammerlock

(3) Toe-hold

(4) Full Nelson

Third Period of 30 Days (6 Drills)

Teach Division C, plus training on Perfection of Divisions A & B Defense

(1) Double Wristlock

(2) Double Armlock and Roll

(3) Hammerlock from underneath

(4) Switch from underneath

Each sport is selected to develop qualities desired in the pilot. Boxing, Wrestling and Rough and Tumble, Ju-Jitsu, are for attack and self-defense with instructions in the realities of warfare; in other words, no rules. Drills in football, basketball and track to develop quick acting, coordination of mind, eye and body, and agility. Military sports will consist of obstacle climbing, grenade throwing, broad jumping, vaulting, tumbling, etc. The swimming courses should be very comprehensive, not only teaching the students to stay afloat but to be familiar and relaxed in the water; to be able to swim with clothes on, disrobe, and life-save.

3. The second 45-minute drill will have the groups reversed; the two companies having sports in the first drill changing to hard labor, etc. and the companies coming from labor take the selected sports.

4. The last 20-minute period provides for students to cool off, get showers, and shift to dry clothes. This is essential to keep the students from colds, etc.

(c) <u>Military Drills</u>

The military drills are divided into two parts also; the battalion is divided, each two companies forming a group and alternating on the two drills listed as follows:

1. <u>Infantry Drill.</u> A period of one hour - 5 min. daily devoted to drill under arms, landing force, etc.

2. <u>Military Arts Drill.</u> The whole group (2 companies) will take 15 min. of radio, semaphore, or blinkers drill each day. Then the group will split into platoons in the following tentative subjects:

    (a) Seamanship
    (b) Gunnery - use of pistol, rifle, machine gun, AA gun
    (c) Rifle range
    (d) Use of parachute
    (e) Chemical Warfare
    (f) First Aid
    (g) Getting out of jungle
    (h) Recognition of silhouettes

(d)   Naval Lore - 45 minutes

  1.

Group A.
- 1st week - Organization of the Navy, customs, etc.
- 2nd week - Regulations
- 3rd week - Naval History
- 4th week - Elements of the Navy - Types of ships, purposes, characteristics, marines, aircraft, etc.

Group B.
- 5th week - Fundamental subjects of Navy; Engr., Nav., Gun, etc.
- 6th week - Fleet functions and basic strategy
- 7th week - Enemy Organization and Military Forces
- 8th week - Opposing World Order - Ideologies, Nationalistic attitudes, Force vs. Right, Economic strength and weakness, Propaganda.

Group C.
- 9th week - History of Military and Naval Aviation
- 10th week - Functions and Tactics of types of aircraft
- 11th week - Enemy tactics - develop hate, etc.
- 12th week - Essentials of victory - mastery of weapon - determination, physical fitness, etc.

  2.   Ground School Subjects - 45 minutes

    (a) Mathematics
    (b) Navigation
    (c) Meteorology
    (d) Seamanship
    (e) Physics
    (f) Gunnery

  3.   Study Period - 45 minutes

It is particularly desirable that the course in Naval Lore be purposeful and comprehensive. Not only give the students a necessary background of naval information, etiquette, and tradition, but to imbue each one with a deep determination to carry out his duties and responsibilities with an aim for perfection. Also, indoctrinate him into wartime thinking, building hate for our enemies and their methods, teaching him it is a privilege to die for his country's cause, cultivating the reckless, devil-may-care spirit.

This type of teaching is far more important than the mere study of certain subjects. This training should start at the Induction Center and be steadily built throughout the whole flight training course. It is believed that our present training system occupies the student's mind so completely with the maze of unquestionably necessary technical subjects that the basic motives to destroy our enemies are left to develop as they may. Our nation's whole line of reasoning has been allowed to develop along this trend, so that we find ourselves mere "babes in arms" in this highly essential characteristic for war. For the above reasons I recommend that some of the country's best practical psychologists be employed to work on this phase, and that one or more suitable psychologists be employed on the staffs of all naval air training bases to work on the planting in the pilots and crews minds consciously or unconsciously this vital wartime psychology.

Also a psychiatrist should be employed at each Induction Center to deal with some "misfits" that undoubtedly will be inducted.

(e) <u>Varsity, Intramural and Voluntary Sports</u>

The last period of two hours in the afternoon will be devoted to compulsory participation in Varsity, Intramural or Voluntary Sports.

All the work during the daily program has been for individual perfection and development. It is firmly believed that the best all-round sports development for war rests in highly competitive team games. Therefore, while the student will have a choice of his activity during this period, that choice will be in a highly organized program of competitive team sports, providing fun as well as developing a fighting spirit. A compulsory hike will effectively drive each boy into some activity.

The program of sports must be closely woven, well integrated, one emphasizing both Varsity and Intramural athletics.

Varsity sports are considered very desirable for many reasons. The competitive spirit is developed to a much higher degree than in Intramural games. Any competitor will hit a stranger harder than his own friends or schoolmates. The standard of perfection is higher, the test of skill and character are desirably sterner. The benefits in morale are infinitely greater for the whole student body for they derive more pride and satisfaction from their interest in a Navy team than in the localized doing of "Company D."

Furthermore, these Varsity sports will provide much valuable publicity and interest for the general public and should arouse a great interest in the boys of the schools of our country who are our potential pilot material and who I believe will "go" for this whole program in a big way. The caliber and scope of inter-collegiate athletics will undoubtedly fall off, so thus the Navy has an excellent chance to capitalize on the situation.

In this connection I recommend that the Secretary be requested to appoint an Advisory Council of the leading Sports Writers and Sports Radio Announcers for this Naval Aviation Physical Program. Such men as **Grantland Rice would be** delighted to serve, and their lead in placing this program before the public will be very beneficial, especially from a procurement of Cadets standpoint.

The contemplated list of Varsity and Intramural sports follows with the number of students expected on each varsity squad, and the number of men from each Platoon who will be expected to participate in the Company and Platoon competition, which will constitute the Intramural program:

	Varsity		Intramural	Competition	No. from Platoon
Fall & Spring	Football (90) Soccer (60)	Fall & Winter	Basketball Touchball	- Plat. - Plat.	(10) (18)
Winter	Basketball (30) Boxing (30) Wrestling (30)	Spring & Summer	Softball Volleyball	- Plat. - Plat.	(18) (10)
Summer	Baseball (30) Track (60)				
Year Round	Swimming (30)	Year Round	Soccer Boxing Wrestling	- Company - Company - Company	(7) (5) (5)

The above is a rough estimate or sample pattern only. It is assumed that about 5 men from each Platoon will participate in Varsity Sports. The other 45 men are accounted for in the intramural system. This does not include tennis, squash, handball or other individual sports which will probably be used in a degree equal to the facilities. The sports indulged in will depend somewhat on the geographic location of the Center. Hockey and Skiing will no doubt be popular and beneficial in northern climates.

The Varsity and Intramural sports must be closely linked so that the number of sports in each field will provide the exercise and recreation for the mass of boys each day.

(f) A ten minute period is provided daily for chapel. It is contemplated that one or two "fighting parsons" will be assigned each Center, and that each day the Cadets will have time for singing one hymn, and receive the benefit of spiritual inspiration in the form of a five minute talk with a "barb" in it.

(g) A rest period of 30 minutes after lunch is considered advisable to allow the Cadets to digest their lunch, relax, and rest between the strenuous morning and afternoon schedules. They should be confined to the quiet of their rooms for this period.

(h) The time after supper of about one hour and 20 minutes should be varied and somewhat optional. Possibly two or three nights a week study periods may be scheduled. When these occur a short period of 20 to 30 minutes should be provided before taps, so that the Cadets may be able to blow off a little steam if they have any left. The other nights should be devoted to light, carefree recreation consisting of movies, touring radio troupes, basketball games, boxing and wrestling meetings, etc. It is possible that some of the educational films of the Navy can profitably be shown at these times. A competent recreation officer should have the responsibility of arranging this entertainment.

(i) Eight hours of sleep are necessary.

The best designed diet possible should be supplied these Cadets. Good food and plenty of it will be needed by the students to supply them with the energy to go through their day's work and to assist in the building up of strong bodies. Good morale is a direct benefit obtained from hard work and good food. Each Center should have a nutritional expert on its staff, and the best men in the country on the subject should be called in as consultants so that the students will obtain the maximum in physical strength from the food provided. Such a diet cannot be maintained on the regular Navy ration allowance. It will be necessary to appropriate additional funds for this purpose.

The medical staff should be carefully selected for these centers. Competent doctors are necessary. However, their governing policy must be the same as the rest of the Centers, namely: to produce strong, tough men and, outside of necessary treatments, there will be no moddlecoddling of these Cadets. Certain injuries are inevitable in such a program, but due to precautions for safety having been taken, the whole program should not be allowed to slow down by fear of contracting injuries among a small minority of the students, thus softening the mental attitude of the majority. In addition to a regular sick bay or hospital staff, one or two sports physicians should be attached to the athletic staff to administer to the bruises, sprains, etc., as well as to consult on matters of posture, instruct in matters of camp hygiene, etc. A staff of trainers should work under the direction of these sports doctors. At the risk of being branded for heresy, I further recommend that one of these sports doctors be an osteopath, or one fully acquainted with osteopathy methods.

9. A series of practical physical tests will be conducted at the induction of each Cadet and periodically throughout his year's training to determine his initial condition, strength, posture and physical defects, and to note his progress as he advances in his training. A record card will be kept on the Cadet to follow his progress. The weight of each man will be recorded weekly.

10. The uniforms for this training program can be the same as are now used with the addition of drill suits for the physical training. A special uniform is considered necessary for this work. Exercise and drills will be conducted with Cadets clad only in trunks and proper footwear when weather conditions permit. At other times it is believed that a washable workout suit similar to the "sweat suits" for basketball teams would be most practicable. These suits should have a tough exterior surface similar to "gabardine football pants" with a light fleece lining. Each cadet should probably have three or four of these suits in order to present a clean appearance. A heavy marching shoe will be necessary in addition to a sturdy athletic shoe.

11. Each Induction Center will need large quantities of athletic equipment; and necessary personnel to order, account, maintain, repair, and issue this equipment will form an important part in the athletic staff. It is probable that a great deal of equipment may be taken over in the lease of the colleges, but this program will call for large quantities of material beyound that on hand at any university and an immediate survey is necessary to ascertain the needs, availability and necessity of priorities in manufacture of certain necessary items, such as rubber goods. An example is the need for mats and rubberized cover for the work in wrestling above.

12. An organization diagram is attached as Enclosure (A). A rough estimate of the staff at each Induction Center is listed below based on the above plan, and for ease of computation on a student body of 1800 men:

Executive Position	Rank		
Commandant	Commander	1	
Executive Officer	Lt. Commander	<u>1</u>	2

ATHLETIC DEPARTMENT

Athletic Director	Lt. Comdr.	1	
Head of Sports	Lt. Comdr. or Lt.	1	
Sport Coaches	Lieut.	8	
Assistant Sport Coaches (for each sport)	Lt. (j.g.)	24	
Head of Intrumurals	Lt. Comdr. or Lt.	1	
Assistants	Lt. (j.g.)	3	
Head of Physical Fitness	Lt. Comdr. or Lt.	1	
Assistants	Lt. (j.g.)	3	
*Physical Instructors (1 per Platoon)	Ensign or C.P.O.	36	
Head of Equipment	Lieut.	1	
Assistants	Ensign or C.P.O.	3	
Chief Master at Arms	C.P.O.	1	
Groundskeepers, etc.	Laborers	8	
Trainers	??	<u>2</u>	93

*Alternate with Military Platoon Commander weekly

ACADEMIC DEPARTMENT

Naval Lore - (12 concurrent classes - 36 classes daily)

Head of Department	Lt. Comdr.	1	
Executive Officer	Lt.	1	
Instructors	Lt. Lt. (j.g.) or Ensign	<u>18</u>	20

Ground School

Head of Department	Lt. Comdr.	1	
Executive Officer	Lieut.	1	
Instructors	Lt. Lt. (j.g.) or Ensign	<u>18</u>	20

Specialties

Head of Department	Lieut.	1
Executive Officer	Lt. (j.g.)	1
Ordnance Officers	Lt. (j.g.)	3
Ordnance Instructors	Enlisted	12
Seamanship Officers	Lt. (j.g.)	3
Seamanship Instructors	Enlisted	12
Parachute Instructors	Enlisted	3
Chemical Warfare Instructors	Enlisted	3
Signal Instructors	Enlisted	9
Radio Instructors	Enlisted	18
Study Monitors	Lt. (j.g.)	3	68

TOTAL 108

MILITARY & DRILL DEPARTMENT

Head of Department	Lt. Comdr.	1
Battalion Commanders	Lieut.	3
Company Commanders	Ensigns	12
*Platoon Commanders	Ensigns or C.P.O.	36
Drill Instructors and Rifle Range	(Gun Sgt. USMC)	12	64

*Alternate with Physical Fitness Instructors weekly

ADMINISTRATIVE DEPARTMENT

Medical Department

Head of Department	Lt. Comdr.	1
Doctors	Lieut.	3
Dentists	Lt. or Lt. (j.g.)	3
Sports Doctors	Lieut.	2
Nutrition Expert	Lt. Comdr. or Lt.	1	10

Supply Department

Head of Department	Lt. Comdr.	1
Commissary Officers	Lieut. & Lt. (j.g.)	2
Stores Officers	Lieut.	1
Disbursing Officer	Lt. (j.g.)	1	5

Buildings and Grounds

Head of Department	Lieut.	1
ASSISTANTS	Ensigns	2	3

Specialists

Chaplain	Lt. Comdr. or Lt.	1	
Psychologist	Lieut.	1	
Psychiatrist	Lieut.	1	
Recreation Officer	Lieut.	1	
Public Relations Officer	Lieut.	1	
Band Leader	C. P. O.	1	
Band	Enlisted	45	51

TOTAL 69

GRAND TOTAL 336

Plus:

Service Staff

Janitors, Waiter, Baker, Groundskeepers, Laundry, Storekeepers, Yeomen, Pharmacist Mates, Nurses, etc.

13. The strength and virility of the entire staff of these Centers will play a vital part in the molding of our new pilots, and must be carefully selected. These men, especially the physical instructors, should be examples of clean living, rugged manhood and possess enthusiasm and a tough spirit. As far as possible, emphasis should be placed on selecting men who are practical and experienced in teaching boys to face stern competition. Our instructors must be able to command the respect of the Cadets while working with them shoulder to shoulder, and exhibit a brand of leadership which will soon make the cadets able to accept responsibilities. Every effort should be made to secure Naval men of the right kind for the indoctrination work. The atmosphere of these Centers should be as naval as possible. Great emphasis should be laid on the ambition for pilot's wings and naval aviation be built up at every turn. A number of naval aviators should be brought in regularly to lecture to the Cadets.

14. It will be necessary to hold a school for the instructors. All the school instructors should be indoctrinated thoroughly in the job to be done, and learn to speak the same language and strive for the same goal. The more they know about the Navy the better the job they will do. If possible, this indoctrination school should be held at the Naval Academy, where so much can be gained by mere association. The school routine may be tried out on the instructors first and many of the bugs may be worked out. Civilian instructors should be checked for pacifistic or communistic leanings before employed. Willingness to cooperate should be a large consideration.

15. There are many items to work into the training which have not been mentioned. It is contemplated that long hikes will be made so that our Cadets can march 30 or 40 miles in a day at the conclusion of training. Methods to live and get out of a jungle, rules for talking if taken prisoner, and many other small subjects can be covered. A thorough system of processing Cadets by means of I. Q's., personal interviews and other tests can be installed.

16. Practically no liberty is planned for these Cadets during this period. Liberty can be held out as a reward for intramural competition, and thus serve as an incentive. It is believed that a monastic life at the Induction Center will produce the best results, and the tougher and more Spartan-like the atmosphere the better fighters the pilots will be. The atmosphere is so important in these centers, the work so concentrated, the building up of Cadets bodies and minds so essential that it is considered almost imperative that these Centers be established by themselves in a small community and as far away from the influences of our country's peace time life as possible. We cannot afford to have these pilots play second fiddle to anybody, least of all on the campus of their Induction Centers.

17. The physical training program at the Reserve Bases, Advanced Training Bases, and Operation Bases will be designed to tie in with the above program and be adapted to the other training taking place at each base. A study to present methods must be made, and steps taken to continue a modified physical training program adjusted to the other work at those stations. The physical fitness program should be established as an integral part of the training at all stations and not be left to the whims of each Commanding Officer. Facilities and machinery must be provided so that exercise is made readily available. The main problem is to break down the habits of the Navy from the past and present toward physical fitness and win it over to a necessary practical system.

18. This program must reach beyond the one year's flight training. The tremendous good of this program will lose its value if allowed to slip away as soon as the pilot leaves training. Athletic facilities should be added in the fleet and at all stations to make it easy for personnel to keep fit and relaxed. The over-all program and that for the other type bases will be submitted later after the immediate problem of the Induction Centers is settled.

19. Applications received to date and other indications make it apparent that we can select the very best personnel in the nation's athletic system to work on this program.

The outline as stated above is only a preliminary survey of the situation and it is contemplated calling in some of the best equipped men in the country to confer and give counsel on the plan. It is believed that this basic program is feasible and can be effectively placed into operation. The program fills a vital need, and it is hoped that little compromise will be necessary in order that close to 100% of value may be attained.

T. J. Hamilton
Lt. Comdr. USN
Division of Aviation Training

Index

to

Interviews with

Rear Admiral Thomas J. Hamilton
U. S. Navy (Retired)

ATHLETICS IN THE NAVY: Hamilton talks about present day need for greater emphasis on competition in sports, p. 23-6;

BORRIES, Capt. Fred (Buzz) Jr.: the great navy halfback (1934), p. 27;

BRYANT, Bear: University of Alabama coach, p. 51-52;

CLIFTON, RADM Jos. C.: p. 9;

COACHING: Hamilton comments on the subject, p. 32-33;

ComAirPac: late 1944 Hamilton returns to Pearl Harbor on staff as Training Officer for Admiral Towers and later Adm. Montgomery, p. 101-3;

CUTTER, Captain Slade D.: the great navy tackle (1934), p. 27-28;

USS ENTERPRISE: Hamilton joins her in May, 1943, p. 75; p. 76; John Crommelin serves as Executive, p. 76; ship engages in widespread use of catapulting, p. 77; Hamilton's job was planning operations from the ship, p. 79; various operations in which she participated, p. 80-4; Hamilton becomes Executive, p. 88; p. 93; Hamilton leaves ship in Dec. 1944, p. 96; story of Adm. Reeves and Jerry Flynn, p. 97-8; Hamilton has temporary command of ship, p. 99-100; p. 101;

U. S. FLEET TEAM (FOOTBALL): Hamilton coaches the Fleet Team for three seasons - on leave from the LEX and the MILWAUKEE, p. 20 ff; Hamilton's comments on the need for a highly developed athletic program in the navy today, p. 23-6;

GARDNER, RADM J. M.: skipper of ENTERPRISE, p. 91; p. 97; p. 99; as Rear Admiral comes back to fly flag in ENTERPRISE, p. 101;

HALSEY, Flt. Admiral Wm. F. Jr.: p. 87; p. 90-1; Hamilton lauds Halsey, p. 92-3 p. 99;

HAMILTON, Howard: Dean at Ohio State University - brother of Thomas - applied system of eytraining to a course in RECOGNITION, p. 54;

HAMILTON, Rear Admiral Thomas J.: Background, p. 1; his abiding interest in sports leads him to the Naval Academy, p. 2-6; awards and honors during his academy years, p. 6 ff; aviation summer (1927), p. 8; his marriage (1932), p. 73-4; after post war (WW II) duty at the Naval Academy he goes in 1949 as Athletic Director to the University of Pittsburg, p. 108 ff; his retirement from active career in 1971, p. 113-4; Football Hall of Fame (1965), p. 114; Football Foundation Gold Medal to recognize contribution of the Navy's sports program in WW II, p. 114; other sports awards, p. 114-5;

HEYWARD, VADM Alexander S. (Sandy), p. 37-8;

INGRAM, Bill: brother of Admiral Jonas Ingram - also a football coach at Academy, p. 4; Hamilton becomes his assistant in fall of 1927, p. 9; p. 12; becomes coach at University of California (Berkeley) p. 21;

INGRAM, Adm. Jonas H.: Director of Athletics at Naval Academy, p. 4; p. 116;

JAMES, Capt. George S. (Buck) Jr.: on duty as transport pilot at NAS Anacostia (1941) - flies Winston Churchill from Norfolk to Anacostia in Lockheed Lodestar, p. 46-9;

KANE, Capt. R. F. (Killer): pilot on ENTERPRISE, p. 80; p. 83; p. 84-5;

KESSING, RADM O. O. (Scrappy): p. 63; his work in setting up bases in Pacific area, p. 99;

KING, Fleet Admiral Ernest J.: skipper of the LEXINGTON, the fleet exercise, p. 14-15; fleet airwing commander (1937-9), p. 36-40;

MARTIN, VADM Wm. I.: Squadron commander, torpedo planes, ENTERPRISE, p. 78-81; p. 84; his work in developing night flying techniques, p. 100-1;

USS MARYLAND: Hamilton reports as junior officer (1927), p. 10; Hamilton coaches at Naval Academy in fall of 1928 and then returns to MARYLAND until Oct. 1929, p. 10-12;

USS MILWAUKEE: Hamilton transfers (1933) to a scouting squadron aboard her, p. 17 ff; p. 26;

N. A. S. ANACOSTIA: Duties of Hamilton and other pilots stationed there, p. 45-6;

U. S. NAVAL ACADEMY: Hamilton stays on after graduation (June 1927) as Assistant football coach under Bill Ingram, p. 8-9; Hamilton returns to Academy in 1928 to serve as Assistant Football Coach, p. 10; Hamilton back to Academy (fall of 1930) as Assistant Coach under Ingram, p. 11-12; Hamilton ordered back to serve as head football coach (1934), p. 26; roster of outstanding players in 1934, p. 27-8; Hamilton starts a recruiting program for football players at Naval Academy, p. 30; Adm. Fitch calls Hamilton back as head football coach during seasons of 1946 and 1947, p. 106-7; Hamilton becomes Athletic Director, p. 108 ff;

NAVAL AVIATION: Aviation summer at USNA (1927), p. 8; Hamilton reports to Pensacola for flight training (Oct. 1929), p. 11-12; Hamilton has aviation instruction duties at N.A. while serving as head football coach (1934-5), p. 29-30;

NCAA: Hamilton serves as first chairman of their TV committee in 1950, p. 109-110; Hamilton also served as chairman of their committee on fitness, p. 110; committee on drug abuse, p. 113; the football rules committee, p. 115;

NICHOLSON, Bill: a talented football player - rejected by Naval Academy because he was color blind, p. 30-31;

O'HARE, Lt. Comdr. Edward Henry (Butch): his loss from the ENTERPRISE, p. 77-8; he had inaugurated the use of 'BAT' teams of night fighters with radar in their wings, p. 78;

U. S. OLYMPIC COMMITTEE: Hamilton serves for sixteen years (1948-64), p. 111;

PACIFIC EIGHT CONFERENCE: Hamilton served for twelve years (beginning in 1959) as Commissioner for the Pacific Eight Conference, p. 112; Administration of the Rose Bowl Game, p. 112;

PREFLIGHT SCHOOLS AND PHYSICAL TRAINING SECTION: p. 52; Hamilton put in charge - selection of 2,500 officers out of 25,000 applicants - the syllabus on physical training, p. 52; the Craighead twins and their book on survival training, p. 53; Coaches recruiting teams, p. 55; the system of training schools under the Radford program, p. 57-8; obtaining personnel - Naval Academy grads in civilian life, p. 59-60; sites of pre-flight schools, p. 60; p. 62; training of air crewmen, p. 62; experiments at Harvard with various tests on physical fitness, p. 69-70; war record of the V-5 officers, p. 72; as Training Officer at ComAirPac (1944-5) Hamilton discovers value of the Preflight schools, p. 102-3; p. 105;

RADFORD, Admiral Arthur: as Director of Naval Aviation and Training he wanted to use competitive athletics to increase abilities of combat pilots for the Navy, p. 50; he sends Hamilton to NCAA meeting and to the American Football Coaches Association to see if good coaches could be recruited for this purpose, p. 51; Hamilton ordered to staff of Radford in charge of Preflight Schools and the Physical Training Section, p. 52; Radford's wisdom in extending the training period, p. 59; p. 65;

REEVES, Admiral J. W. Jr. (Blackjack): p. 97-8;

RENSHAW, Sam: psychologist at Ohio State University - applies his Recognition system to the training of navy personnel, p. 54; p. 68;

ROOSEVELT, Eleanor: Hamilton has lunch with her - enlists her support to save the Preflight schools' football schedules with U. S. Colleges, p. 66-67;

ROOSEVELT, President F. D.: meets Churchill at NAS Anacostia (1941), p. 48-49;

USS SAVO ISLAND (CVE-78): Hamilton becomes skipper shortly after VJ day, p. 105-6;

TOMLINSON, Comdr. Wm. G. (Red): C.O. of VP-9; p. 38-9; p. 44; duty as NAS, Anacostia, p. 45;

TORPEDO SQUADRON #1: on board USS LEXINGTON (Jan. 1931) p. 12; a fleet exercise with King as skipper of the LEX, p. 13-14;

TUNNEY, Lt. Comdr. Gene: in charge of physical training program for the Navy - disturbed at Hamilton's efforts to recruit coaches for pilot training, p. 63-5; p. 67;

ULITHI: The Naval base, p. 98-9;

VP-9: (patrol) Hamilton leaves N.A. Jan. 1937 - joins VP-9 in San Diego, p. 34 ff; a resume of duties, p. 1937-9, p. 35; Adm. King as fleet airwing commander insists on improving instrument flying, p. 36-40; a gunnery school established, p. 41-2; excellence in bombing and machine gun practices, p. 42-3;

www.ingramcontent.com/pod-product-compliance
Lightning Source LLC
Chambersburg PA
CBHW080612170426
43209CB00007B/1412